Kaplan Publishing are constantly finding r
difference to your studies and our excitin
offer something different to students loo

CW01068520

This book comes with free MyKaplan onli
study anytime, anywhere. **This free onlir
separately and is included in the price of the book.**

Having purchased this book, you have access to the following online study materials:

CONTENT	ACCA (including FBT, FMA, FFA)		FIA (excluding FBT, FMA, FFA)	
	Text	Kit	Text	Kit
Electronic version of the book	✓	✓	✓	✓
Check Your Understanding Test with instant answers	✓			
Material updates	✓	✓	✓	✓
Latest official ACCA exam questions*		✓		
Extra question assistance using the signpost icon**		✓		
Timed questions with an online tutor debrief using clock icon***		✓		
Interim assessment including questions and answers	✓		✓	
Technical answers	✓	✓	✓	✓

* Excludes BT, MA, FA, FBT, FMA, FFA; for all other papers includes a selection of questions, as released by ACCA
** For ACCA SBL, SBR, AFM, APM, ATX, AAA only
*** Excludes BT, MA, FA, LW, FBT, FMA and FFA

How to access your online resources

Kaplan Financial students will already have a MyKaplan account and these extra resources will be available to you online. You do not need to register again, as this process was completed when you enrolled. If you are having problems accessing online materials, please ask your course administrator.

If you are not studying with Kaplan and did not purchase your book via a Kaplan website, to unlock your extra online resources please go to www.mykaplan.co.uk/addabook (even if you have set up an account and registered books previously). You will then need to enter the ISBN number (on the title page and back cover) and the unique pass key number contained in the scratch panel below to gain access. You will also be required to enter additional information during this process to set up or confirm your account details.

If you purchased through the Kaplan Publishing website you will automatically receive an e-mail invitation to MyKaplan. Please register your details using this email to gain access to your content. If you do not receive the e-mail or book content, please contact Kaplan Publishing.

Your Code and Information

This code can only be used once for the registration of one book online. This registration and your online content will expire when the final sittings for the examinations covered by this book have taken place. Please allow one hour from the time you submit your book details for us to process your request.

Please scratch the film to access your unique code.

TsjS-ZSGq-1wTX-Rp5N

Please be aware that this code is case-sensitive and you will need to include the dashes within the passcode, but not when entering the ISBN.

KAPLAN

PUBLISHING

ACCA Diploma in Financial and Management Accounting (RQF Level 2)

FA1

Recording Financial Transactions

EXAM KIT

British Library Cataloguing-in-Publication Data

A catalogue record for this book is available from the British Library.

Published by Kaplan Publishing UK

Unit 2 The Business Centre

Molly Millar's Lane

Wokingham

Berkshire

RG41 2QZ

ISBN: 978-1-78740-872-2

© Kaplan Financial Limited, 2021

Printed and bound in Great Britain.

Acknowledgements

These materials are reviewed by the ACCA examining team. The objective of the review is to ensure that the material properly covers the syllabus and study guide outcomes, used by the examining team in setting the exams, in the appropriate breadth and depth. The review does not ensure that every eventuality, combination or application of examinable topics is addressed by the ACCA Approved Content. Nor does the review comprise a detailed technical check of the content as the Approved Content Provider has its own quality assurance processes in place in this respect.

This product contains material that is ©Financial Reporting Council Ltd (FRC). Adapted and reproduced with the kind permission of the Financial Reporting Council. All rights reserved. For further information, please visit www.frc.org.uk or call +44 (0)20 7492 2300.

We are grateful to the Association of Chartered Certified Accountants for the permission to reproduce past examination questions. The answers have been prepared by Kaplan Publishing.

INTRODUCTION

Packed with practice and exam-type questions, this book will help you to successfully prepare for your exam.

- All questions are grouped by syllabus topics with separate sections for 'study support questions' (Section 1 of this book) and 'multiple choice questions' (Section 2).

- The study support questions (in section 1) are designed to test your understanding of the syllabus topics. These can be attempted either during your initial study or your early revision phase. In the approach to the exam you should turn your focus away from these to the exam style multiple-choice questions to gain exam practice.

- The multiple choice questions (in section 2) are all in exam style and of exam standard. You should ensure that in the last few days/weeks of your preparation before the exam you focus exclusively on this style of question to ensure you are sufficiently rehearsed in this style of question.

- A mock exam is provided at the back of the book. You should try this under timed conditions and this will give you an idea of how you will perform in your exam.

ENHANCEMENTS

We have added the following enhancement to the answers in this exam kit:

Tutorial note

Some answers include tutorial notes to explain some of the technical points in more detail.

CONTENTS

Quality and accuracy are of the utmost importance to us so if you spot an error in any of our products, please send an email to mykaplanreporting@kaplan.com with full details.

Our Quality Co-ordinator will work with our technical team to verify the error and take action to ensure it is corrected in future editions.

INDEX TO QUESTIONS AND ANSWERS

KAPLAN PUBLISHING

SYLLABUS AND REVISION GUIDANCE

SYLLABUS CONTENT

A TYPES OF BUSINESS TRANSACTION AND DOCUMENTATION

1 Types of business transaction

(a) Understand a range of business transactions including:

    (i) sales

    (ii) purchases

    (iii) receipts

    (iv) payments

    (v) petty cash

    (vi) payroll

(b) Understand the various types of discount including where applicable the effect that trade discounts have on sales tax.

(c) Describe the processing and security procedures relating to the use of:

    (i) cash

    (ii) cheques

    (iii) credit and debit cards

    (iv) debit cards for receipts and payments and electronic payment methods.

2 Types of business documentation

(a) Outline the content of a range of business documents to include but not limited to:

    (i) invoice

    (ii) credit note

    (iii) remittance advice

(b) Prepare the financial documents to be sent to credit customers including:

    (i) sales invoices

    (ii) credit notes

    (iii) statements of account.

(c) Prepare remittance advices to accompany payments to suppliers.

(d) Prepare a petty cash voucher including the sales tax element of an expense when presented with an inclusive amount.

3   Process of recording business transactions within the accounting system

(a)   Identify the characteristics of accounting data and the sources of accounting data records, showing understanding of how the accounting data and records meet the business' requirements.

(b)   Understand how users can locate, display and check accounting data records to meet user requirements and understand how data entry errors are dealt with.

(c)   Outline the tools and techniques used to process accounting transactions and period-end routines and consider how errors are identified and dealt with.

(d)   Consider the risks to data security, data protection procedures and the storage of data.

(e)   Understand the principles of coding in entering accounting transactions including:

(i)   describing the need for a coding system for financial transactions within a double entry bookkeeping system

(ii)   describing the use of a coding system within a filing system.

(f)   Code sales invoices, supplier invoices and credit notes ready for entry into the books of prime entry.

(g)   Describe the accounting documents and management reports produced by computerised accounting systems and understand the link between the accounting system and other systems in the business.

B   DUALITY OF TRANSACTIONS AND THE DOUBLE ENTRY SYSTEM

1   Books of prime entry

(a)   Outline the purpose and content of the books of prime entry including their format.

(b)   Explain how transactions are entered in the books of prime entry.

(c)   Outline how the books of prime entry integrate with the double entry bookkeeping system.

(d)   Enter transactions including the sales tax effect where applicable into the books of prime entry.

2   Double entry system

(a)   Define the accounting equation.

(b)   Understand and apply the accounting equation.

(c)   Understand how the accounting equation relates to the double entry bookkeeping system.

(d)   Process financial transactions from the books of prime entry into the double entry bookkeeping system.

3   The journal

(a)   Understand the use of the journal including the reasons for, content and format of the journal.

(b)   Prepare journal entries directly from transactions, books of prime entry as applicable or to correct errors.

4   Elements of the financial statements

(a)   Define and distinguish between the elements of the financial statements.

(b)   Identify the content of a statement of financial position and statement of comprehensive income.

C   BANK SYSTEM AND TRANSACTIONS

1   The banking process

(a)   Explain the differences between the services offered by banks and banking institutions.

(b)   Describe how the banking clearing system works.

(c)   Identify and compare different forms of payment.

(d)   Outline the processing and security procedures relating to the use of cash, cheques, credit cards, debit cards for receipts and payments and electronic payment methods.

2   Documentation

(a)   Explain why it is important for an organisation to have a formal document retention policy.

(b)   Identify the different categories of documents that may be stored as part of a document retention policy.

D   PAYROLL

1   Process payroll transactions within the accounting system

(a)   Prepare and enter the journal entries in the general ledger to process payroll transactions including:

(i)   calculation of gross wages for employees paid by the hour, paid by output and salaried workers

(ii)   accounting for payroll costs and deductions

(iii)   the employer's responsibilities for taxes, state benefit contributions and oth deductions.

(b)   Identify the different payment methods in a payroll system, e.g. cash, che automated payment.

(c)   Explain why authorisation of payroll transactions and security of payroll inf is important in an organisation.

E   LEDGER ACCOUNTS

1   Prepare ledger accounts

(a)   Enter transactions from the books of prime entry into the ledgers.

(b)   Record journal entries in the ledger accounts.

(c)   Balance and close off ledger accounts.

F   CASH AND BANK

1   Maintaining a cash book

(a)   Record transactions within the cashbook, including any sales tax effect where applicable.

(b)   Prepare the total, balance and cross cast cash book columns.

(c)   Identify and deal with discrepancies.

2   Maintaining a petty cash book

(a)   Enter and analyse petty cash transactions in the petty cash book including any sales tax effect where applicable.

(b)   Balance off the petty cash book using imprest and non imprest systems.

(c)   Reconcile the petty cash book with cash in hand.

(d)   Prepare and account for petty cash reimbursement.

G   SALES AND CREDIT TRANSACTIONS

1   Recording sales

(a)   Record sales transactions taking into account:

    (i)   various types of discount

    (ii)   sales tax

    (iii)   the impact of the sales tax ledger account where applicable

(b)   Prepare the financial documents to be sent to credit customers.

2   Customer account balances and control accounts

(a)   Understand the purpose of an aged receivable analysis.

(b)   Produce statements of account to be sent to credit customers.

(c)   Explain the need to deal with discrepancies quickly and professionally.

(d)   Prepare the receivables control account or receivables ledgers by accounting for:

   (i)   sales

   (ii)   sales returns

   (iii)   payments from customers including checking the accuracy and validity of receipts against relevant supporting information

   (iv)   discounts

   (v)   irrecoverable debt and allowances for irrecoverable debts including any effect of sales tax where applicable.

H   PURCHASES AND CREDIT TRANSACTIONS

1   Recording purchases

(a)   Record purchase transactions taking into account:

   (i)   various types of discount

   (ii)   sales tax effect

   (iii)   the impact of the sales tax ledger account where applicable

(b)   Enter supplier invoices and credit notes into the appropriate book of prime entry.

2   Supplier balances and reconciliations

(a)   Prepare the payables control account or payables ledgers by accounting for:

   (i)   purchases

   (ii)   purchase returns

   (iii)   payments to suppliers including checking the accuracy and validity of the payment against relevant supporting information

   (iv)   discounts

I   RECONCILIATION

1   Purpose of control accounts and reconciliation

(a)   Describe the purpose of control accounts as a checking devise to aid management and help identify bookkeeping errors.

(b)   Explain why it is important to reconcile control accounts regularly and deal with discrepancies quickly and professionally.

2   Reconcile the cash book

(a)   Reconcile a bank statement with the cash book.

3   Reconcile the receivables control account

(a)   Reconcile the balance on the receivables control account with the list of balances.

4   Reconcile the payables control account

(a)   Reconcile the balance on the payables control account with the list of balances.

J   PREPARING THE TRIAL BALANCE

1   Prepare the trial balance

(a)   Prepare ledger balances, clearly showing the balances carried down and brought down as appropriate.

(b)   Extract an initial trial balance.

2   Correcting errors

(a)   Identify types of error in a bookkeeping system that are disclosed by extracting a trial balance.

(b)   Identify types of error in a bookkeeping system that are not disclosed by extracting a trial balance.

(c)   Use the journal to correct errors disclosed by the trial balance.

(d)   Use the journal to correct errors not disclosed by the trial balances.

(e)   Identify when a suspense account is required and clear the suspense account using the journal.

(f)   Redraft the trial balance following correction of all errors.

PLANNING YOUR REVISION

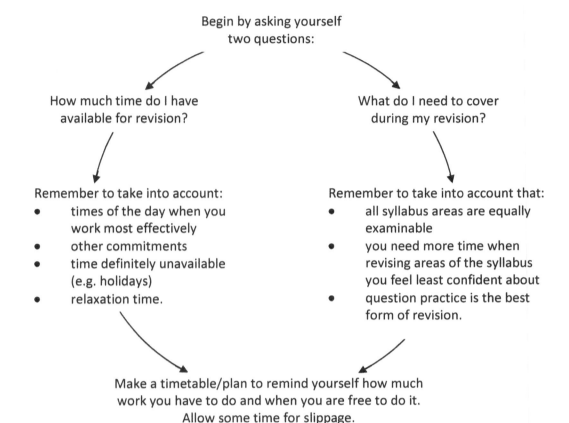

Begin by asking yourself
two questions:

How much time do I have
available for revision?

What do I need to cover
during my revision?

Remember to take into account:
- times of the day when you
  work most effectively
- other commitments
- time definitely unavailable
  (e.g. holidays)
- relaxation time.

Remember to take into account that:
- all syllabus areas are equally
  examinable
- you need more time when
  revising areas of the syllabus
  you feel least confident about
- question practice is the best
  form of revision.

Make a timetable/plan to remind yourself how much
work you have to do and when you are free to do it.
Allow some time for slippage.

REVISION TECHNIQUES

- Go through your notes and study text highlighting the important points
- You might want to produce your own set of **summarised notes**
- **List key words** for each topic to remind you of the essential concepts
- **Practise exam-standard questions**, under timed conditions
- **Rework questions** that you got completely wrong the first time, but only when you think you know the subject better
- If you get stuck on topics, **find someone to explain** them to you (your tutor or a colleague, for example)
- **Read recent articles** on the ACCA website or in the student magazine
- **Read** good newspapers and professional journals

THE EXAM

FORMAT OF THE EXAM

The exam is a computer-based exam.

	Number of marks
50 multiple-choice questions (2 marks each)	100
Time allowed: 2 hours	

Answering the questions

- **Multiple-choice questions** – read the questions carefully and work through any calculations required.

- **If you don't know the answer**, eliminate those options you know are incorrect and see if the answer becomes more obvious. Remember that only one answer to a multiple choice question can be right!

- **If you get stuck with a question** skip it and return to it later.

- **Answer every question** – if you do not know the answer, you do not lose anything by guessing. Towards the end of the examination spend the last five minutes reading through your answers and making any corrections.

- **Equally divide the time** you spend on questions. In a two-hour examination that has 50 questions you have about 2.4 minutes per a question.

- **Do not skip any part of the syllabus** and make sure that you have *learnt* definitions, *know* key words and their meanings and importance, and *understand* the names and meanings of rules, concepts and theories.

- Bear in mind that this exam questions that test your understanding of narrative and computational elements, so ensure that you are able to deal with both types of question.

Computer-based examinations

- Be sure you understand how to use the **software** before you start the exam. If in doubt, ask the assessment centre staff to explain it to you.

- Questions are **displayed on the screen** and answers are entered using keyboard and mouse. At the end of the exam, you are given a certificate showing the result you have achieved.

- **Don't panic** if you realise you've answered a question incorrectly – you can always go back and change your answer.

ACCA SUPPORT

For additional support with your studies please also refer to the ACCA Global website.

Section 1

STUDY SUPPORT QUESTIONS

BUSINESS TRANSACTIONS AND DOCUMENTATION

1   CASH OR CREDIT

Given below are a number of transactions. For each transaction, tick the relevant box to indicate whether it is a cash transaction or a credit transaction.

TRANSACTION		CASH	CREDIT
(a)	Receipt of goods worth $140.59 from a supplier together with an invoice for that amount.		✓
(b)	Payment of $278.50 by cheque for a purchase at the till.	✓	
(c)	Receipt of a deposit of $15.00 for goods.	✓	
(d)	Sending of an invoice for $135.00 to the payer of the deposit for the remaining value of the goods.		✓
(e)	Sale of goods for $14.83, payment received by credit card.	✓	

(5 marks)

2   DOCUMENTS

Fill in the boxes to give the names of the various documents used at the following stages of the process of purchasing goods by means of cash or on credit.

(a)	Request to supplier to supply goods.	order
(b)	Notification by supplier of the amount due to be paid for the goods.	purchase invoice
(c)	Notification by purchaser to the supplier of the amount enclosed as payment.	remittance advice
(d)	Cancellation of an amount due to a supplier	credit note
(e)	Record of a cash sale given to a customer.	cash receipt

(5 marks)

3   DEBIT/CREDIT NOTES

Fill in the gaps in the following sentences, which explain the difference between a debit note and a credit note.

[handwritten: supplier]   *[handwritten: customer]*

A credit note is a document produced by the .... and sent to the .... which cancels all or part of ...*[handwritten: an INVOICE]*...

[handwritten: customer]   *[handwritten: supplier]*

[handwritten in margin: credit note]

A debit note, on the other hand, is raised by the ....and sent to the .... requesting a .... Not all businesses employ a formal debit note for this purpose; many rely on a letter or telephone call only.

(6 marks)

DOUBLE ENTRY BOOKKEEPING

4   TERMINOLOGY

Fill in the gaps to identify the following terms:

(a)   An ...*[handwritten: asset]*... is a present resource controlled by the ...*[handwritten: entity]* as a result of a past...*[handwritten: events]*.

(b)   A ...*[handwritten: liability]*...is an amount owed by the business to another business or individual. Examples include a ...*[handwritten: loan from bank]* and amounts owed to the suppliers of goods or services which have yet to be paid for.

(c)   ...*[handwritten: Inventory]*... is an asset comprising goods purchased for resale, components for inclusion in manufactured products, and the finished products which have been manufactured which have not yet been sold.

(d)   ...*[handwritten: Capital]* is the liability of the business to the owner of the business.

(e)   ...*[handwritten: Drawings]*is the term which refers to amounts taken out of the business by the owner.

(10 marks)

5   CLASSIFYING TRANSACTIONS AND BALANCES

Given below are a number of typical transactions and balances that might be found in a business.

Fill in the boxes to indicate whether the items are assets, liabilities, expenses or income.

(a)   Goods stored in the warehouse awaiting resale   *[handwritten: Assets]*

(b)   Electricity bill paid   *[handwritten: Expenses]*

(c)   Cash received from sale of goods   *[handwritten: Income]*

(d)   Amounts owing from a customer *[handwritten: receivables]*   *[handwritten: Asset]*

(e)   Rent paid for the factory building   *[handwritten: Expense]*

(f)   Cash paid into the business by the owner   *[handwritten: Liability]*

(g)   Amounts owed to suppliers *payables* | Liability |

(h)   Cash held in the till | Asset |

(i)   Machinery purchased for use in the factory | Asset |

(j)   Rent received for subletting part of the factory premises | Income |

(k)   Cash held in the business bank account . | Asset |

(11 marks)

6   BILL SMITH – ACCOUNTING EQUATION

In the following transactions the accounting equation builds up at each stage.

Use the boxes below the accounting equation to show the amounts in each category in which the transactions would be recorded and what the business owns and owes cumulatively, after each transaction.

(a)   Bill Smith starts a new business by putting $10,000 into a business bank account.

Assets =	Capital	+ Profit	– Drawings	+ Liabilities
10,000	10,000			

(b)   A bank lends the business a further $5,000.

Assets =	Capital	+ Profit	– Drawings	+ Liabilities
15,000	10,000			5000

c) 9,000 @ Bank
6,000 @ Van

(c)   Bill buys a delivery van for $6,000.

Assets =	Capital	+ Profit	– Drawings	+ Liabilities
15,000	10,000			5000

(d)   Bill buys inventory for $2,500 by writing out a business cheque.

Assets =	Capital	+ Profit	– Drawings	+ Liabilities
15,000	10,000			5000

6500 @ Bank
2500 @ Invent
6000 @ Van

(e)   All the inventory is sold for $4,000. The money is paid direct to the business bank account.

(Remember there are two elements to this transaction. Firstly, the money coming into the business and the fact that the business no longer has an inventory asset, and secondly, the calculation of profit.)

Assets =	Capital	+ Profit	– Drawings	+ Liabilities
16500	10000	1500		5000

(f)   Bill pays a business expense of $400 out of the business bank account.

Assets =	Capital	+ Profit	– Drawings	+ Liabilities
16100	10,000	1100		5000

(g)   Finally Bill takes $300 out of the business for his own purposes.

Assets =	Capital	+ Profit	– Drawings	+ Liabilities
15800	10000	1100	300	5000

(16 marks)

7 BANNER'S BOOKS – LEDGER ACCOUNTS

James Banner begins a business as a second-hand bookseller on 1 February 20X7. His first week's transactions are listed below.

(a)   Deposit $5,000 in a business bank account as the opening capital.

(b)   Purchase books for $600, by cheque.

(c)   Sell books for $800 cash.

(d)   Pay rent of $500, by cheque.

(e)   Buy a second-hand van for $2,000, by cheque.

Required:

For each of these transactions indicate which ledger account would be debited and which would be credited in the table given below.   **(5 marks)**

Transactions	Account to be debited	Account to be credited
(a)		
(b)		
(c)		
(d)		
(e)		

8 CAMERON FINDLAY – LEDGER ACCOUNTS

Cameron Findlay opens his fishing tackle shop on 1 June 20X8. During that month he makes the following business transactions:

(a)   Paid $1,500 into a business bank account

(b)   Paid one month's rent of $230

(c)   Purchased rods for $420, by cheque

(d)   Purchased nets for $180, by cheque

(e)   Sold some of the rods for $240 cash

(f)   Purchased live bait for $10, by cheque

(g)   Sold live bait for $16

(h)   Purchased flies for $80, by cheque

(i)   Paid shop assistant's wages of $95

(j)   Sold some of the flies for $50

(k)   Paid sundry expenses of $10

Required:

Record the above transactions in the following ledger accounts.   (11 marks)

+   −

Cash at bank account

Capital 1500	Rent 230
Sales 240	Purchases 420
16	180
50	10
	80
= 1806	Wages 95
	Sundry expenses 10
Balance b/d 781	Balance c/d 781
	1806

Capital account

	Cash at Bank 1500

Rent account

230	

Purchases account

Rods 420	
Nets 180	
Live bait 10	Balance c/d 640
Flies 80	
690	
Balance b/d 640	

Sales account

Balance c/d 306	rods 240
	Live bait 16
	flies 50
	306
	Balance b/d 306

Wages account

95	

Sundry expenses account

10	

9 JOHN FRY – LEDGER ACCOUNTS AND BALANCING

On 14 April 20X5 John Fry set up a business in which he sold frozen fish, meat and vegetable dishes from door to door in a specially adapted van. His transactions for the first two weeks of trading were as follows:

(a) Paid $10,000 of redundancy money into a business bank account

(b) Used $3,600 to buy a second hand van by writing a cheque

(c) Spent $1,700 by cheque having the van converted as a travelling deep freeze

(d) Paid $400 in cash for his first assignment of frozen food

(e) Received $110 of cheques and $80 of cash for sales in his first week of trading

(f) Spent $260 in cash on a back up freezer in which to store additional inventory

(g) Paid $190 in cash for additional inventory

(h) Received $170 of cheques and $50 of cash for sales in his second week of trading

(i) Paid his next door neighbour $40 in cash as wages for help in moving inventory from the freezer to the van

(j) Withdrew $60 in cash from the business bank account as living expenses

Required:

Fill in the boxes with the balance carried down on the following accounts:

Cash and bank account

Capital account D (

Van account C (

Purchases account C (

Sales account D (

Freezer account C (

Wages C (

Drawings C (

Cash and bank account	10,410
Capital account	10,000
Van account	5300
Purchases account	590
Sales account	410
Freezer account	260
Wages	40
Drawings	60

(8 marks)

Tutorial note

You may find it helpful (and useful practice) to answer this question by entering these transactions in the appropriate ledger accounts. Then calculate a balance on each ledger account.

10 **ASSETS OR LIABILITIES?**

Given below is a list of typical assets and liabilities that might be found in a business.

Required:

Fill in the boxes by stating whether each of the following items is either an asset or a liability.

(a) Cars for use by the sales team   `Asset`

(b) Computers for resale   `Asset`

(c) Bank overdraft   `Liability`

(d) Monies owed by a customer   `Asset`

(e) Trade payables   `Liability`

(f) Office furniture   `Asset`

(g) Trade receivables   `Asset`

(7 marks)

BANKING AND PETTY CASH

11   PETTY CASH PRACTICE

On 1 August 20X4 $73.42 of cash was put into the petty cash box to top it up to the imprest amount of $200 and on 8 August a further $114.37 was put into the box in cash. Cash payments during the week ending 7 August 20X4 were evidenced by the following vouchers.

Petty Cash Voucher	No.	279		Petty Cash Voucher	No.	280
Date 1 Aug X4				Date 1 Aug X4		

For what required	AMOUNT $	¢
Tea, coffee, biscuits.	11	78
Signature **J Small**		
Authorised **Petty cashier**		

For what required	AMOUNT $	¢
Taxi	3	90
Signature **P Printer**		
Authorised **Petty cashier**		

Petty Cash Voucher	No.	281		Petty Cash Voucher	No.	282
Date 2 Aug X4				Date 3 Aug X4		

For what required	AMOUNT $	¢
Window cleaner	26	00
Signature **J Small**		
Authorised **Petty cashier**		

For what required	AMOUNT $	¢
Client lunch (including sales tax of $4.16)	27	90
Signature **Rillingworth**		
Authorised **Petty cashier**		

KAPLAN PUBLISHING

Petty Cash Voucher	No.	283		
Date	3 Aug X4			

For what required		AMOUNT $	¢
Stamps		11	00
Signature	J Small		
Authorised	Petty cashier		

Petty Cash Voucher	No.	284		
Date	4 Aug X4			

For what required		AMOUNT $	¢
Boxfiles		12	49
Paper (including sales tax of $2.90)		7	00
Signature	T Semper		
Authorised	Petty cashier		

Petty Cash Voucher	No.	285		
Date	4 Aug X4			

For what required		AMOUNT $	¢
Rail fare		12	00
Signature	J Small		
Authorised	Petty cashier		

Petty Cash Voucher	No.	286		
Date	4 Aug X4			

For what required		AMOUNT $	¢
Stamps		2	30
Signature	T Semper		
Authorised	Petty cashier		

Required:

Complete the petty cash book for the first week in August 20X4 by filling in the shaded boxes overleaf. **(10 marks)**

PETTY CASH BOOK

Date 20X4	Receipts $	Voucher/ reference no	Details	Total payment $	Sales tax $	Office expenses $	Travel expenses $	Postage $	Stationery $	Sundry $
1 Aug	116.58		Balance b/d							
1 Aug	73.42		Cash from bank							
1 Aug		279	Refreshments	11 78		11 78				
1 Aug		280	Taxi	3 90			3 90			
2 Aug		281	Window cleaners	26 00		26 00				
3 Aug		282	Client lunch	27 90	4 16					23 74
3 Aug		283	Stamps	11 00				11 00		
4 Aug		284	Stationery	19 49	2 90				16 59	
4 Aug		285	Rail fare	12 00			12 00			
4 Aug		286	Stamps	2 30				2 30		
				114 37	7 06	37 78	15 90	13 30	16 59	23 74
			Balance c/d	85 63						
7 Aug	200			200 00						
7 Aug	85.63		Balance b/d							
8 Aug	114.37		Cash from bank							

12   IMPREST SYSTEM

Fill in the gaps in the following sentences:

Payments out of petty cash will occur when an authorised _petty cash voucher_ .... and supporting _receipts_ .... are produced. Properly evidenced vouchers are .... _authorised_ by senior members of staff.

At the end of the month the petty cash payments will _equal_ the vouchers and their supporting documentation, and a cheque will be cashed at the bank for this amount so as to replenish the _imprest_

The vouchers etc. will be removed and _filed_ after having been recorded in the _petty cash book_ .... The vouchers, cash and petty cash records are held securely in a box and preferably in a _safe_ ....   **(8 marks)**

13   BANKING SERVICES

Fill in the gaps in the following sentences:

Standing orders and direct debits are both methods of payment whereby the bank is instructed to pay a third party from a bank account. However, the main difference is as follows:

(i)   with a _standing order_ .... it is the payer who instructs his bank to pay a certain amount on a regular basis to the payee

(ii)   with a _direct debit_ .... it is the payee that instructs the bank of the payment and specifies the amount which may alter for each payment.

Credit cards and debit cards are both methods of making payments used by consumers. However the main difference is as follows:

(i)   a _credit c_ .... is a means of purchasing goods without immediate payment. Payment is made on the total balance outstanding on the card sometime after the purchase has been made

(ii)   a _debit c_ .... is a method of making an immediate payment for purchases but without the need to write out a cheque. On payment with a _debit c_ .... the purchaser's bank account is electronically debited immediately with the amount of the purchase.   **(4 marks)**

14   PARTIES TO A CHEQUE

Consider the cheque below:

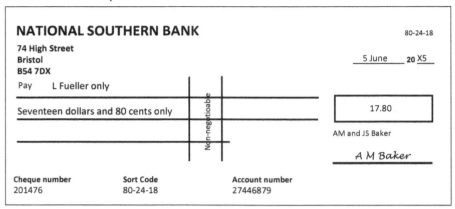

NATIONAL SOUTHERN BANK   80-24-18

74 High Street
Bristol   5 June   20 X5
B54 7DX

Pay   L Fueller only

Seventeen dollars and 80 cents only   17.80

                                             AM and JS Baker

                                             A M Baker

Cheque number   Sort Code   Account number
201476   80-24-18   27446879

Required:

Fill in the boxes with the names of each of the following parties to the cheque:

(a)   the drawer   AM + JS Baker

(b)   the drawee   National Southern Bank

(c)   the payee   L Fueller

(3 marks)

15   BANKING MONEY

Fill in the gaps in the following sentences:

It is important to keep cash, cheques and vouchers secure. If any are lost or stolen, this reduces the profits of the organisation. Initially the various items tend to be kept in a *till* and any excess amount should be regularly transferred to a *safe* during the day, keeping actual cash in the *till* to a minimum. Money, vouchers and so on should also be taken to the *bank* regularly to reduce the amount held on premises. This could be daily, every two or three days or other intervals depending on the amount received day to day. Banking should be undertaken *irregularly* ………………. so that there is not a regular pattern of visiting the bank.

Paying in slips ………………….. are used to include details of cash and cheques and, usually separately, card vouchers. If the business accepts a number of cheques, it is usual to supply a *remittance list* ……………………. which can be checked against the actual cheques by the bank to avoid or resolve problems.

If the home branch of the business is in another city, the amounts paid into the bank will need to travel through the *banking circulation* which takes several days before it reaches the home branch. On receipt, certain items will be 'cleared' such as *cash* ………. This amount can be used immediately. Cheques paid into the bank are subject to clearance before the amount they represent can be used as cleared funds. This period provides sufficient time for the cheques to be returned if there are any technical problems with the cheque or there are *insufficient funds* ……………………. in the account.

If the business has a large number of staff, *BACS* …………. should be used to pay wages and salaries into the bank accounts of the staff members. This reduces the amount of cash that needs to be maintained on the premises and avoids the need to write out numerous cheques or credit transfers.

(10 marks)

16 MAINSTREAM CO – CHECKING CORRECTNESS OF REMITTANCES

You work for an organisation called Mainstream Co. In the post this morning, 12 July, the following remittance advice and cheque were received from one of your customers, Tarbick & Co.

TARBICK & CO

74 Hartston Street, Brinton, SY3 5AZ

Date: 10 July 20X5   **REMITTANCE ADVICE**

Date	Description	Amount
	Inv. 52843	361.30
	Inv. 53124	227.00
	Inv. 53128	450.20
		1,038.50
	Cheque enclosed Cheque no	1,038.50

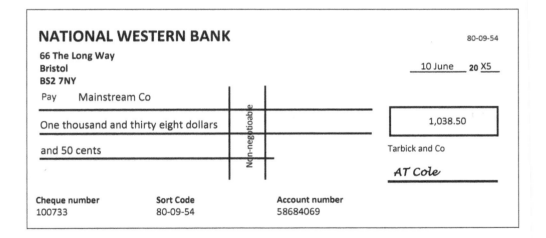

NATIONAL WESTERN BANK   80-09-54

66 The Long Way
Bristol
BS2 7NY   10 June   20 X5

Pay   Mainstream Co

One thousand and thirty eight dollars   1,038.50

and 50 cents   Tarbick and Co

Non-negotioabe   AT Cole

Cheque number	Sort Code	Account number
100733	80-09-54	58684069

The receivables' ledger records for Tarbick & Co show the following position at 12 July:

Outstanding invoices

Date	Number	$
14 June	52843	316.30
27 June	53124	227.00
29 June	53128	450.20
5 July	53317	482.68

Required:

A number of errors have been made on the remittance advice. Fill in the boxes below:

(a)   The invoice number   52843   was for   316·30   rather than the   361·30   entered onto the remittance advice.

(b)   The revised cheque total should be   993·5 .   **(4 marks)**

17   ROBERT DEMPSTER – CASH BOOK

Robert Dempster runs a wholesale business supplying small medical items to chemists' shops, sports clubs and local businesses. All his transactions are on credit. His transactions in the first month of trading are listed below.

(a)   Opened a bank account in the name of Surgical Supplies and deposited $10,000.

(b)   Bought a delivery van for $4,000 from Vans Galore.

(c)   Sold bandages and one box of antiseptic cream to Woodside Rugby Club for $65.

(d)   Paid Vans Galore $2,000 and Surgiplast $150.

(e)   Received a cheque for $65 from Woodside Rugby Club.

(f)   Paid Robert Dempster's private electricity bill of $130.   PEA'RLS

Required:

(a)   Complete the following bank account.

Cash at bank account

	$			$
(a) Capital	10,000	(d) Vans Galore		2,000
(e) Woodside Rugby Club	65	(d) Surgiplast		150
		(f) R.D Electricity		130
		Balance c/d		7,785
	10,065			10,065
Balance b/d	7,765			

(5 marks)

(b)   Fill in the gaps in the following sentences to explain the principles behind the treatment of transaction (f) above.

separate entity

The .... concept is the principle underlying the treatment of the owner's private expenses paid by the business. This concept requires the transactions of a *business*. to be recorded separately from those of the *owners*. of a business. Consequently, this payment could not be analysed as 'electricity' as it is not the electricity expense of the business. It may be thought of as a withdrawal of cash from the business by the owner.   **(5 marks)**

(Total: 10 marks)

P   R
E   L
A   S

SALES AND SALES RECORDS

18   SALES TAX

During the month of March 20X4 a business made sales on credit of $15,790 plus sales tax and purchases on credit of $12,455 inclusive of sales tax. Also during this month $13,612 was received from receivables in cash and cheques and cheque payments of $9,400 were made to payables. Sales tax is at the rate of 17.5%.

Required:

(a)   Write up these transactions by completing the following ledger accounts.   **(9 marks)**

Sales account   *15790 × 17.5% = 2763.25*

	$		$
Bal c/d	15790	Receivables (net)	15790
	15790		15790

Receivables account

	$		$
		Cash	13,612.00
Sales	18553.25	Bal c/d	4,941.25
	18553.25		18553.25

Purchases gross amount 12455
Sales tax = 12455 × 17.5 / 117.5 = 1855
                                    10,600

Purchases account

	$		$
Payables (net)	10,600	Bal c/d	10,600
	10,600		10,600

Payables account

	$		$
Cash	9,400.00		
Bal c/d	3055	Purchases	12,455
	12,455		12,455

Sales tax account

	$		$
Sales tax on purchases	1855		
Bal c/d	908.25	Sales tax on sales	2763.25
	2763.25		2763.25

(b) **Choose the correct option to complete the following sentence:**

The balance on the sales tax account shown above represents the amount of sales tax that is *owing to/repayable by* the taxation authorities. **(1 mark)**

✓

(Total: 10 marks)

19 VICTORIA LTD – POSTING FROM THE SALES DAY BOOK

Given below are the sales day book and details of cash receipts taken from the cash book for Victoria Ltd for the week ended 3 August 20X8.

Required:

You are required to write up the nominal ledger and receivables ledger accounts given from these day books. Victoria Ltd maintains the receivables ledger control account within the double entry system. (Note that you are NOT required to balance the accounts.)

(27 marks)

Sales day book

Date		Invoice no.	Customer name	R/L ref	Gross	Sales tax	Net
					$	$	$
July	30	5102	Cameron Ass	045	48.18	7.17	41.01
	30	5103	AM McGee	027	159.30	23.72	135.58
	31	5104	Peter Rover	026	142.03	21.15	120.88
Aug	1	5105	Olivia Consultants	015	82.47	12.28	70.19
	1	5106	Monty Dee	003	61.48	9.15	52.33
	2	5107	Roberts Partners	007	153.20	22.81	130.39
	2	5108	Anna Pargeter	019	221.78	33.03	188.75
	2	5109	Stephen Williams & Co	001	69.00	10.27	58.73
	3	5110	Owens Ltd	036	159.36	23.73	135.63
	3	5111	Clive Brown	035	62.70	9.33	53.37
					1,159.50	172.64	986.86

Receipts – cash book

Date	Narrative	Folio ref.	Bank		Sales tax		Retail sales		Receivables	
30 July	Anna Pargeter	019	204	30					204	30
	Imogen Jones	009	73	20					73	20
31 July	Cameron Ass	045	37	40					37	40
	Phillipa Steven	032	116	78					116	78
1 Aug	Owens Ltd	036	217	84					217	84
2 Aug	Monty Dee	003	73	50					73	50
	AM McGee	027	190	54					190	54
3 Aug	Roberts Partners	007	111	62					111	62
			1,025	18					1,025	18

Nominal ledger

Sales

	$			$
		30 July	Balance b/d	24,379.20
			SDB	986.86

Receivables ledger control

	$		$
30 July Balance b/d	1,683.08	Receivables	1025.18
SDB	1,159050		

Sales tax

	$		$
		30 July Balance b/d	352.69
		SDB	172.64

Receivables ledger

Stephen Williams & Co   001

	$		$
30 July Balance b/d	38.20		
SDB	69.00		

Monty Dee   003

	$		$
30 July Balance b/d	73.50	Receivables	73.50
SDB	61.48		

Roberts Partners   007

	$		$
30 July Balance b/d	279.30	Receivables	111.62
SDB	153.20		

Imogen Jones			**009**
	$		$
30 July Balance b/d	137.23	Receivables	73.20

Olivia Consultants			**015**
	$		$
30 July Balance b/d	42.61		
SDB	82.47		

Anna Pargeter			**019**
	$		$
30 July Balance b/d	198.17	Receivables	204.30
SDB	221.78		

Peter Rover			**026**
	$		$
30 July Balance b/d	296.38		
SDB	142.03		

AM McGee			**027**
	$		$
30 July Balance b/d	335.28	Receivables	190.54
SDB	159.30		

Phillipa Steven			**032**
	$		$
30 July Balance b/d	116.78	Receivables	116.78

Clive Brown   035

	$		$
30 July Balance b/d	35.10		
SDB	67.70		

Owens Ltd   036

	$	Receivables	217.84
30 July Balance b/d	512.74		
SDB	159.36		

Cameron Associates   045

	$	Receivables	37.40
30 July Balance b/d	335.28		
SDB	48.18		

20   CREDIT LIMITS

Below are some details about customer account balances.

Name	Account	Credit limit	Current balance
		$	$
B T Prim	2143910Z	10,000	8,329.17
ZLT Ltd	1178947A	35,000	17,171.27
P Jones & Co	3419284A	21,000	22,457.75
A M N & Sons	4547448B	3,500	1,117.18
Claridge & Sons	7743914B	2,100	898.89
Foster Ltd	4143725A	7,500	2,379.84
Smith & Co	7143428B	1,700	1,845.45
Rowan Ltd	5671289T	12,000	8,943.71
Cozens & Sons	6143448A	21,000	18,934.21
P J Cartwright	7781821B	1,100	27.94
Alan Thorpe	2247981B	5,000	4,721.97

Required:

(a)   Which two customers have balances exceeding their credit limit?   **(2 marks)**

(b)   Which three customers have credit limits in excess of $20,000?   **(3 marks)**

(c)   Give three examples of action which can be taken to chase outstanding debts.

(3 marks)

(Total: 8 marks)

Action which can be taken to chase outstanding debts can range from reminder letters and telephone calls to legal action and, eventually, taking a decision to write the amount off as a bad debt. Such action must be seriously considered and appropriately authorised by management.

21 LANCING LTD – AGED RECEIVABLES ANALYSIS

Given below are four receivables ledger accounts for Lancing Ltd.

You are required to prepare an aged receivables analysis of these debts on the proforma given below. Today's date is 31 March 20X5. (10 marks)

Vinehall Ltd

		$			$
1 Jan	Opening balance	127.38	15 Jan	Cash	73.57
28 Jan	Invoice 22936	28.36	10 Feb	Cash	117.27
4 Feb	Invoice 22975	117.27			
7 Mar	Invoice 23011	72.48	31 Mar	Closing balance	154.65
		_____			_____
		345.49			345.49
		_____			_____

Handwritten in left margin: ∠90, ∠30

Cranbrook Ltd

		$			$
1 Jan	Opening balance	37.28	12 Jan	Cash	37.28
10 Jan	Invoice 22881	106.27	20 Jan	Cash	106.27
18 Jan	Invoice 22901	128.27	25 Feb	Cash	117.25
15 Feb	Invoice 22999	117.25			
6 Mar	Invoice 23008	115.36			
20 Mar	Invoice 23031	112.35	31 Mar	Closing balance	355.98
		_____			_____
		616.78			616.78
		_____			_____

Skinners Ltd

		$			$
1 Jan	Opening balance	227.71	7 Jan	Cash	172.36
21 Jan	Invoice 22912	103.46			
15 Feb	Invoice	71.62			
20 Feb	Invoice 23002	193.77	31 Mar	Closing balance	424.20
		_____			_____
		596.56			596.56
		_____			_____

Bickley Ltd

		$			$
1 Jan	Opening balance	72.36	10 Jan	Cash	51.26
15 Jan	Invoice 22941	88.20	12 Jan	Credit note C441	21.10
2 Feb	Invoice 22962	56.00	20 Feb	Cash	88.20
28 Feb	Invoice 23007	39.37	13 Mar	Cash	56.00
15 Mar	Invoice 23026	61.32	31 Mar	Closing balance	100.69
		_____			_____
		317.25			317.25
		_____			_____

Aged receivable listing

Customer	< 30 days $	< 60 days $	<90 days $	> 90 days $	Total $
Vinehall Ltd	72.48	–	28.36	53.81	154.65
Cranbrook Ltd	227.71	–	128.27	–	335.98
Skinners Ltd	–	265.39	103.46	55.35	424.20
Bickley Ltd	61.32	39.37	–	–	100.69
Total	361.51	304.76	260.09	109.16	1,035.52

PURCHASES AND PURCHASE RECORDS

22   POSTING CREDIT TRANSACTIONS

During its first month of trading a business has the following transactions:

(a)   Receipt of cash from the owner into a business bank account of $7,300

(b)   Purchases on credit of $460

(c)   Purchases for cash of $120

(d)   Payment of rent in advance of $240

(e)   Sales on credit of $330

(f)   Sales for cash of $220

(g)   Payment of wages of $90

(h)   Receipt of a loan from a friend of the owners of $2,000

(i)   Purchase on credit of furniture (a long term asset) for $560

(j)   Receipts from accounts receivables of $330

(k)   Payments to accounts payables of $570

Required:

For each of these transactions indicate which ledger account would be debited and which would be credited in the table given below.   **(11 marks)**

Transactions	Account to be debited	Account to be credited
(a)	BANK	CAPITAL
(b)	Purchases	Accounts payable
(c)	Purchases	Bank
(d)	Rent	Bank
(e)	Accounts receivable	Sales revenue
(f)	Bank	Sales revenue
(g)	wages	Bank
(h)	Bank	Loan
(i)	Furniture	Accounts payable
(j)	Bank	Accounts Receivable
(k)	Accounts payable	Bank

23   SETTLEMENT DISCOUNTS

A business received an invoice for the purchase of goods totalling $600 with the offer of a 3% settlement discount for early payment. The business paid early to take advantage of the early settlement discount.

The same business issued an invoice to one of its customers for $900 with a 3% settlement discount if it is paid before the normal settlement date. This customer normally takes advantage of the early settlement discount, and the sales invoice was prepared on that expectation. Subsequently, the customer paid within the required time to be eligible for the discount.

Required:

Using the following T accounts, record all the transactions above from initial invoices through to payment and dealing with the settlement discounts.   **(6 marks)**

Ignore sales tax.

Accounts receivable

Sales 873	Cash @ Bank 873	

Sales account

	Accounts Receivable 873

Accounts payable

Cash@Bank 582	Inventory 600
Discounts 18	

Discounts received

	Accounts Payable 18

Purchases account

Accounts Payable 600

Cash at bank account

Accounts Receivable 873 | Accounts payable 582

24 GEER & CO – POSTING FROM THE PURCHASE DAY BOOK

Given below is the purchase day book and cash payments from the cash book for Geer & Co for the week ended 12 May 20X8.

You are required to write up the transactions for the week in the nominal ledger account and payables ledger accounts given. Geer & Co maintains the payables ledger control account within the double entry system.

(Note that you are NOT required to balance the accounts.)   (16 marks)

Purchase day book

Date	Invoice no.	Customer name	P/L ref.	Gross $	Sales tax $	Net $
May 8	G228	Hopkins Ltd	008	128.39	19.12	109.27
9	82456	Flute Brothers	017	48.26	7.18	41.08
9	2294	BA Johnson	012	33.71	5.02	28.69
10	29145	PGE Ltd	015	105.29	15.68	89.61
10	X8/09	Brass & Co	021	51.26	7.63	43.63
12	02268	AD Gosling	003	28.70	4.27	24.43
12	0135	Priddle & Sons	025	60.26	8.97	51.29
				455.87	67.87	388.00

Cash payments – Cash book

Date	Cheque no. $	Supplier	PL code	Total
8 May	03362	Brass & Co	021	37.90
8 May	03363	Hopkins Ltd	008	102.64
10 May	03364	SC Basson	023	93.59
12 May	03365	Rutland Ltd	006	149.37
12 May	03366	PGE Ltd	015	93.70
				477.20

NOMINAL LEDGER:

Purchases

	$		$
8 May Balance b/d	1,652.30		
PDB	388.00		

Payables ledger control

	$		$
CPB	477.20	8 May Balance b/d	912.36
		PDB	455.87

Sales tax

	$		$
PDB	6787	8 May Balance b/d	80.41

PAYABLES LEDGER:

AD Gosling   003

	$		$
		8 May Balance b/d	21.73
		PDB	28.70

Rutland Ltd   006

	$		$
CPB	149.37	8 May Balance b/d	149.37

Hopkins Ltd   008

	$		$
CPB	102.64	8 May Balance b/d	198.37
		PDB	128.39

BA Johnson   012

	$		$
		8 May Balance b/d	–
		PDB	33.71

PGE Ltd   015

	$		$
CPB	93.70	8 May Balance b/d	117.38
		PDB	105.79

Flute Brothers   017

	$		$
		8 May Balance b/d	88.29
		PDB	48.76

Brass & Co   021

	$		$
		8 May Balance b/d	37.90
		PBD	51.26

SC Basson   023

	$		$
CPB	93.59	8 May Balance b/d	93.59

Priddle & Sons   025

	$		$
		8 May Balance b/d	–
		PDB	60.26

25   RETURNING GOODS

Iqbal received a delivery of goods and on unpacking them he thinks that they are not what he ordered. Fill in the gaps in the following sentences to explain what action he should take to check and, if they are not what was required, how he should proceed.

Iqbal must check that his recollection is correct by referring to the .... *original order* This could be a copy of a *written* .... order, a note of a *telephone* order or an *email* confirmation of an order over the internet. If he is right, he should *contact the supplier* to ensure that the correct goods are delivered and the unwanted ones taken back. If there is a delay in delivering the correct goods, he should ask the suppliers to provide a *credit note* so that he will not be charged for the unwanted goods.   **(6 marks)**

PAYROLL

26   PAYROLL KNOWLEDGE

Tick the relevant box to indicate whether each of the following statements is true or false.

		TRUE	FALSE
(a)	State benefit contributions must usually be deducted from amounts paid to employees.	✓	
(b)	All employees are entitled to a written statement of the terms and conditions of employment.		✓
(c)	The responsibilities of an employee are limited to what is specifically required of him in his contract.		✓
(d)	State benefit contributions and income tax records may be discarded once the tax year is finished.		✓

(4 marks)

27   GROSS PAY – SALARIED AND PIECEWORK

472.22
250.00

Fill in the following boxes:

(a)   Henry is a monthly paid employee. On 21 June his annual salary was increased from $8,500 to $9,000. His gross pay on the pay day at the end of June is ⟨722.22⟩.

(b)   Eliza is paid on a piecework basis at the rate of $0.85 for every 10 units produced. In one week her production was as follows:

	Units produced	
Monday	110	
Tuesday	130	630 / 10 = 63
Wednesday	120	
Thursday	140	63 × 0.85 = 53.55
Friday	130	

Her gross pay for the week is ⟨53.55⟩.

(c) In the following week Eliza is told that in addition to her basic piecework rate she will be paid a bonus for any units produced in excess of 650 units per week. The bonus will amount to $1.05 for every 10 excess units.

Her production in this week was as follows:

Units produced

		Units produced
Monday	$700/10 \times 0.85 = 59.5$	135
Tuesday		140
Wednesday	$50/10 \times 1.05 = 5.25$	140
Thursday		150
Friday		135

(handwritten: 700)

Her gross pay for the week is ⟦ 64.75 ⟧.   **(5 marks)**

28 GROSS PAY – OVERTIME

(handwritten: Overtime rate = 7.60 × 1.5 = 11.4)
(handwritten: 14820 / 52 / 37.5 = 7.60)

Fill in the following boxes:

(a) Sandra works a 37½-hour week for an annual salary of $14,820. She is expected to work overtime of up to five hours per week without extra pay, but overtime hours in excess of this are paid at time and a half. *(handwritten: 285 + 45.6)*

(handwritten: 14820/52   4 × 11.4 = 45.6)

In one week she worked 46½ hours. Her gross pay for the week is ⟦ 330.60 ⟧

(b) Chandra has worked seven hours of overtime on top of his usual 35 hour week. Calculate his overtime pay on each of the following assumptions:

(i) His normal rate of pay is $5.20 per hour and all overtime is paid at time and a half. ⟦ 54.60 ⟧ *(handwritten: Overtime pay = 7 × 5.20 × 1.5)*

(ii) His normal rate of pay is $5.20 per hour and overtime is paid at the rate of time and a quarter for the first four hours overtime per week, and at time and a half thereafter. *(handwritten: 4 hours overtime = 4 × 5.20 × 1.25 = 26)* ⟦ 49.40 ⟧

(handwritten: 3 hours overtime = 3 × 5.20 × 1.5 = 23.4) ⟦ 38.50 ⟧

(iii) His annual salary is $10,010 and all overtime is paid at basic rate.

(handwritten: 10,010 / 52 / 35 = 5.5)   **(9 marks)**

29 PAYSLIP

(handwritten: 7 × 5.5 = 38.50)

List five items which might appear on employee's payslip.   **(5 marks)**

(handwritten: employers name, the date, the net pay, total tax for current pay day, the total gross pay for this payday.)

30 PAYROLL ACCOUNTS

State the typical accounts which are used in payroll.   **(5 marks)**

(handwritten:)
- *Wages and salaries expense*
- *Wages and salaries control*
- *The tax authorities*
- *Pension payable*
- *Various non-statutory deductions*

CONTROL ACCOUNTS, BANK RECONCILIATIONS AND THE INITIAL TRIAL BALANCE

31 PHILPOTT AND SONS – SELECTING TRANSACTIONS FOR BANK RECONCILIATION

Listed below are a number of items which account for the difference between the bank statement balance and the cash at bank account balance in the nominal ledger of Philpott and Sons on 31 October 20X8.

Tick the relevant box to show which of the following items would require adjustment in the cash book and which would appear as reconciling items on the bank reconciliation statement. (5 marks)

ITEM		CASH BOOK	BANK RECONCILIATION
(a)	A standing order for $230 appeared on the bank statement but had not been recorded in the cash book.	✓	
(b)	A cheque for $70 written and posted to a supplier on 29 October did not appear on the bank statement until 5 November 20X8.		✓
(c)	A dishonoured cheque for $143 was debited on the bank statement but was not returned to Philpott and Sons until 3 November 20X8.	✓	
(d)	The bank deducted an amount of $27 on 30 October 20X8 in respect of a standing order which had been cancelled on 1 October 20X8 in accordance with bank procedures.		✓
(e)	The cash and cheques banked on 31 October did not appear on the bank statement.		✓

32 PREPARING A BANK RECONCILIATION STATEMENT

(a) A company's cash book shows a balance of $2,369.37 on 31 May 20X4.

The bank statement recently received as at 31 May 20X4 does not include cheque payments of $394.67 and payments into the bank account totalling $936.03.

A direct debit for $393.60 appeared on the bank statement but was not entered in the cash book.

The closing balance on the bank statement at 31 May is $1,434.41.

Required:

Complete the following cash account and bank reconciliation statement at 31 May 20X4. (4 marks)

Bank reconciliation statement at 31 May 20X4

	$
Balance per bank statement	1,434.41
Less:	394.67
Add:	936.03
Balance per cash book (working)	1975.77

Working:

Cash at bank account

	$		$
Balance b/d	2,369.37		
	2,369.37		393.60
Balance b/d	1975.77	Balance c/d	1975.77

(b) **Fill in the gaps in the following sentences which explain why bank reconciliation statements should be prepared regularly.**

The regular preparation of bank reconciliations serves as a check on both the organisation's records and those of the bank.

The bank reconciliation may highlight differences between the bank statement and the cash book and these can then be investigated and the organisation's and bank's records brought up to date.

Bank reconciliations also serve as a check on the time taken to bank lodgements and for them to clear through the banking system.

Finally cheques that have been drawn but not yet presented can also be monitored in this way.   **(6 marks)**

(Total: 10 marks)

33 ANDREWS LTD – RECONCILING THE RECEIVABLES LEDGER CONTROL ACCOUNT

At 30 November 20X5 the balance on the receivables ledger control account of Andrews Ltd totalled $25,390.27. Unfortunately when the individual receivable accounts in the receivables ledger were balanced and totalled this total came to $24,993.57. The accounts were investigated and the following errors were discovered:

(a) The account balance for P Hull totalling $227.40 was omitted from the total of individual receivable balances.

(b) An invoice for $372.19 to M Skinner was posted to the account of H Skinner in error.

(c) An invoice to M Catt for $58.64 has been entered in the sales day book as $85.64.

(d) A debt due from J Callard of $169.30 has been written off as an irrecoverable debt in J Callard's individual receivables ledger account but not in the nominal ledger.

Required:

You are required to complete the following receivables ledger control account balance and to reconcile this corrected balance with the amended total of individual receivables.

(5 marks)

Receivables ledger control

	$		$
30 Nov Balance b/d	25,390.27	31 Mar Error ~~27~~	27
		irrecoverable debts	169.30
		Balance c/d	25,193.97
	25,390.27		25,390.97

Total of receivable balances

	$
Original total	24,993.57
P Hull omitted	227.40
Transposition error	(27)
Amended total	25,193.97

34 A CLIENT – PREPARING A PAYABLES CONTROL ACCOUNT

You have been completing the year end accounts of a client and have the following data:

(i)   Total payables balances   –   per control account $42,578

       –   per list of balances $44,833

(ii)   A credit note for $372 has been received from a supplier but has not been recorded in the Purchases Returns Book.

(iii)   A credit balance of $2,597 has been included in the list of balances as $2,579. 18

(iv)   Standing order payments to a supplier totalling $3,000 have not been recorded in the cash book.

(v)   An account with a debit balance of $700 has been included in the list of balances as a credit balance. 700 × 2

(vi)   A supplier has agreed to write off a balance of $27 as discount. The necessary entry has been made in the supplier's account, but no other entry has been made.

(vii)   An error was made in totalling the invoices in the purchases day book. The total was undercast by $900.

Required:

(a)   Complete the following Payables control account, incorporating the adjustments required in respect of the information above.   (5 marks)

(b)   Complete the following reconciliation of the list of the balances to the revised balance on the control account.   (4 marks)

(Total: 9 marks)

Payables ledger control account

	$			$
Credit Note	372	(i)	Balance b/f	42,578
Standing order	3000		undercast	900
Discount received	27			
Balance c/f				
	40,079			
	43,478			43,478

Reconciliation of the list of balances

		$	$
(i)	Payables balances per list of balances		44,833
	Add: undercast balance		18
	Less: Standing order	3000	
	credit note	372	
	Debit balance as credit	1400	4,772
	−700×2		40,079

35 JUDITH KELLY – CORRECTING THE RECEIVABLES LEDGER CONTROL ACCOUNT

Judith Kelly has extracted and listed the balances on her customers' personal accounts, but the total of the list does not agree with the balance on the receivables ledger control account in her general ledger.

You have obtained the following information from an examination of her records:

(i)   the total of the list of balances is $122,409

(ii)   the balance on the receivables ledger control account in the general ledger is $120,539

(iii)   an account balance of $7,540 (debit) has been included in the list as $5,740 (debit)

(iv)   goods with a value of $2,648 were returned by a customer, and a credit note was issued. The credit note was posted to the personal account, but no other entries were made

(v)   a credit balance of $3,289 has been included in the list as a debit balance

(vi)   Judith agreed to accept a payment of $9,000 in full settlement of a balance of $9,010 due from a customer as a goodwill gesture. The balance on the personal account was cleared, but the amount written off has not been recorded in the nominal ledger

(vii)   a credit balance of $500 has been omitted from the list

(viii) during the year, one of Judith's customers went into liquidation. The balance due ($750) was written off as irrecoverable in the personal ledger, but no entries were made in the general ledger.

Required:

(a) Complete the following receivables ledger control account to show how it would appear after making the necessary correcting entries.   (4 marks)

(b) Show the necessary adjustments to the following list of balances.   (3 marks)

(Total: 7 marks)

Receivables ledger control account

		$		$
(ii)	Balance b/f	120,539	Goods returned	2,648
			written off	10
			irrecoverable	750
			Balance c/d	117,131
		─────		─────
		120,539		120,539
		─────		─────

Adjustments to list of personal balances

	$	
List of personal account balances	122,409	
Transposition error	1,800	
credit as a debit	(6,578)	(3,289 × 2)
omitted from list	(500)	
	─────	
Total of personal account balances	117,131	
	─────	

36 JANE MARSHALL – LEDGER ACCOUNTS AND TRIAL BALANCE

Jane Marshall has set up trading on 5 June 20X9 by paying $6,200 into a business bank account. Her early transactions are as follows:

(a) Sale on credit for $441

(b) Purchase on credit for $237

(c) Payment of rent by cheque of $180

(d) Sale on credit for $118

(e) Sale for cash of $52

(f) Purchase on credit of $162 ✓

(g) Payment of wages in cash of $56

(h) Purchase for cash of $66

(i) Sale on credit of $97

(j) Payment to payables totalling $237 ✓

(k) Withdrawal of $100 in cash by the owner

(l) Receipt from receivables totalling $215

(m) Receipt of a loan of $1,000 from the bank.

Required:

Complete the following trial balance.

Note that you may find it helpful (and useful practice) to produce your workings in T-account format.

Trial balance as at...

	$	$
Cash and bank	6,826	
Capital		6200
Sales		708
Receivables	441	
Purchases	465	
Payables		162
Rent	180	
Wages	56	
Drawings	100	
Loan		1,000
	8,070	8,070

(Total: 28 marks)

37 K MOLE – ERRORS IN THE BOOKS

An organisation that has both a receivables ledger control account and individual receivable accounts in the receivables ledger has discovered the following errors. Fill in the gaps in the following sentences to explain the effect of the errors.

(a)   An invoice to J Mole is entered in the sales day book as an invoice to K Mole.

This is an error of COMMISSION It must be corrected by debiting J Mole and crediting K Mole.

(b)   An invoice to R Fisher has been omitted from the sales day book completely.

This is an error of OMISSION If an invoice has been omitted completely from the sales day book then it will appear nowhere in the accounting records. This means that in the nominal ledger both Sales and receivables will be understated. In the receivable ledger R Fisher's account balance will also be too small as the invoice will not have been entered into his individual account.

(c)   The sales tax column of the sales day book has been overcast by $1,000.

If the sales tax column of the sales day book has been overcast by $1,000 then the sales tax account will have been credited with $1,000 too much and the balance on the sales tax account will therefore be overstated by that amount. There will be no effect on the individual accounts as the error is one affecting the day book totals only.   receivables

(d)   The discount received column in the cash payments book has been undercast by $10.

If the discount received column has been undercast by $10 then the double entry posting in the n̦o̦m̦i̦n̦a̦l̦ ledger for discounts received will be $10 too small. This means that the balance on the discount received account will be $10 too small and the remaining balance on the payables ledger control account will be $10 too l̦a̦r̦g̦e̦. There will be no effect on the individual payables accounts as the error is one concerning totals to the nominal ledger only.

(e)   An invoice to T Toad for $135 has been entered into the sales day book as $153.

In this case the invoice has been entered into the sales day book at an amount of $18 greater than its correct value. This will mean that the postings to the nominal ledger are $18 too great. Therefore the șa̦l̦e̦ș account balance and r̦e̦c̦e̦i̦v̦a̦b̦l̦e̦ș control account balance will both be o̦v̦e̦r̦șța̦țe̦d̦ by $18. The incorrect figure of $153 would also have been used to post the individual receivable account for T Toad. Therefore the balance on T Toad's individual account will also be $18 too great.

(f)   An invoice for $100 plus sales tax at 17.5% to S Waterrat has been entered into the sales day book at simply $100 and the sales tax has been totally omitted.

The posting of $100 to sales in the nominal ledger will be c̦o̦r̦r̦e̦c̦ț. The omission of the sales tax should be corrected by d̦e̦b̦i̦ți̦n̦g̦ the receivables ledger control account and c̦r̦e̦d̦i̦ți̦n̦g̦ the sales tax account. The individual account for S Waterrat should also show the gross total of $117.50.   **(18 marks)**

38   ERROR CORRECTION – JOURNAL

Given below are a number of errors and omissions that have been discovered in the books of an organisation.

(a)   An invoice to P James for $145.79 has been entered into the individual receivables ledger account of P Jones.

(b)   An invoice to H Howitt for $240 plus sales tax at 17.5% has been omitted from the sales day book.

(c)   An invoice for $45.60 to M Pickering has been entered into the sales day book as $54.60. This invoice is for goods that are zero rated for sales tax purposes.

(d)   G Fletcher owes the organisation $250 and is owed in turn $300 by the organisation. It has been agreed that these individual receivable and payable balances should be netted off against one another.

(e) $269.47 owing from J Cook is to be written off as an irrecoverable debt.

Required:

Fill in the gaps in the following journal to correct these items. **(13 marks)**

	Date		Details	Dr $	Cr $
			JOURNAL		
(a)	3/3/X5		P. James	145.79	
			P. Jones		145.79
(b)	3/3/X5		Receivables ledger control	282	
			Sales tax		42
			Sales		240
(c)	3/3/X5		Sales	9	
			Receivables ledger control		9
(d)	3/3/X5		G Fletcher – Payable ledger account	250.00	
			G Fletcher – Receivable ledger account		250.00
			Payable ledger control	250.00	
			Receivable ledger control		250.00
(e)	3/3/X5		Irrecoverable debt expense	269.47	
			Receivable ledger control		269.47

39 ERASMUS – SUSPENSE ACCOUNT

A trial balance for Erasmus is extracted. Debit balances total $165,100; credit balances $157,590. The difference is posted to a suspense account.

Checks are made to discover the reasons for the errors and the following errors are discovered:

(1) No entry has been made for a cash receipt of $600 from an account receivable.

(2) Salaries totalling $3,600 have been posted to travelling expenses

(3) A debit balance on sundry expenses, $860, has been included on the trial balance as a credit balance

(4) The purchases account has not been totalled correctly. The debit column should have been $345,000 and not $357,200

(5) Cash sales receipts have been debited to cash as $3,460 and credited to sales revenue as $6,430. The correct amount is $4,360.

Required:

(a)   Complete the following suspense account.   **(4 marks)**

(b)   For errors (1) and (2), state the type of error discovered.   **(2 marks)**

(Total: 6 marks)

Suspense account

	$			$
(4) Purchases	12,200		Balance b/d	7,510
....	*357,200 - 345,000*	(3)	Sundry expenses *860 × 2*	1,720
		(5)	Cash *4360 - 3460*	900
	12,200	(5)	Sales revenue	2,070
			6430 - 4360	12,200
....				....
	―――			―――

Section 2

MULTIPLE-CHOICE TEST QUESTIONS

BUSINESS TRANSACTIONS AND DOCUMENTATION

1   Which of the following transactions is likely to occur on a daily basis in a large business organisation?

A   Credit sales

B   Payroll ✓

C   Purchase of equipment

D   Payment of suppliers

2   Which of the following comprises small cash transactions?

A   Payments to service providers

B   Petty cash ✓

C   Purchases of inventory

D   Receipts from sales

3   What is the purpose of a credit note?

A   It acknowledges a purchase on credit

B   It is a reference from an agency detailing the creditworthiness of a new customer

C   It is issued when a deposit is paid on goods ✓

D   It is issued to cancel all or part of a sales invoice

4   Which of the following is NOT an internal document for purchases?

A   Supplier list

B   Delivery note ✓

C   Goods received note

D   Purchase order

5   What is a remittance advice for?

Ⓐ   To indicate items now paid

B   To identify goods received   ✓

C   To advise remittances received

D   For notification of goods dispatched

6   What is the purpose of a purchase invoice?

(i)   To claim back the sales tax

(ii)   To identify the goods bought

(iii)   To record how much is owed to the supplier

(iv)   To record how much is owed from the customer

Ⓐ   (i), (ii) and (iii) only

B   All   ✓

C   (ii) and (iii) only

D   (i) and (ii) only

7   In the purchasing procedure, which document will usually follow the goods received note?

A   Delivery note

Ⓑ   Invoice   ✓

C   Statement

D   Advice note

8   Keith received a document from Cullen's Stationery Supplies for eight reams of paper which they supplied three days ago. How would Keith refer to this document?

A   It is a goods received note

B   It is a receipt   ✓

Ⓒ   It is a purchase invoice

D   It is a credit note

9   What is the prime document used to record petty cash transactions in the petty cash book?

A   An invoice

B   A till receipt   ✓

C   A petty cash I.O.U.

Ⓓ   A petty cash voucher

10   Which of the following is a source document for financial transactions?

Ⓐ   Statement

Ⓑ   Paying in slip –   ✕

C   Delivery note

D   Goods received note

11   Which of the following is authorised so that a business can settle an outstanding invoice?

A   A credit note

B   A debit note   ✓

C   A remittance advice

Ⓓ   An internal cheque requisition

12   Which of the following is an advice of employee earnings?

A   Advice note

Ⓑ   Payslip   ✓

C   Purchase order

D   Quotation

13   How will a sales invoice from a supplier be regarded by their customer?

A   As a credit note

B   As a debit note   ✓

Ⓒ   As a purchase invoice

D   As a receipt

14   Why must a business retain documents?

A   Because it has always been done

B   For historical purposes   ✓

Ⓒ   It is a requirement of tax law

D   To facilitate planning

15   Why does data protection legislation exist?

A   To ensure that information is maintained on employees   ✓

B   To preserve records in business for a period of time

Ⓒ   To prevent businesses holding personal information without legitimate reason

D   To specify the records to be maintained in respect of information technology

16 Which of the following items of personal data is excluded from the scope of typical data protection laws?

A Data maintained regarding individual personal suppliers, such as contact details and account history

B Data maintained regarding employees, such as employment history and contact details

C Data maintained regarding individual personal customers, including contact details and account history

(D) Personal data maintained for domestic purposes ✓

DOUBLE ENTRY BOOKKEEPING

17 Horace started a business by paying $5,000 into a business bank account.

What are the accounting entries required to record this?

A	Dr	Capital	$5,000
	Cr	Bank	$5,000
(B)	Dr	Bank	$5,000
	Cr	Capital	$5,000	✓
C	Dr	Bank	$5,000
	Cr	Drawings	$5,000
D	Dr	Drawings	$5,000
	Cr	Bank	$5,000

18 Andrea started a taxi business by transferring her car, worth $5,000, into the business.

What are the accounting entries required to record this?

A	Dr	Capital	$5,000
	Cr	Car	$5,000
B	Dr	Car	$5,000
	Cr	Drawings	$5,000
(C)	Dr	Car	$5,000	✓
	Cr	Capital	$5,000
D	Dr	Car	$5,000
	Cr	Bank	$5,000

19 Jones' account is shown below:

Jones

		$			$
1 January	Bal b/d	250	17 January	Returns out	50
12 January	Sales	1,000	28 January	Bank	800
23 January	Sales	500	31 January	Bal c/d	900
		─────			─────
		1,750			1,750
		─────			─────
1 February	Bal b/d	900			

What is the balance on Jones' account as at 31 January?

A   Debit $250

B   Debit $1,750

C   Debit $900 –

D   Credit $900

20 Which of the following changes could **NOT** occur as a result of an entry in the bookkeeping records?

A   Increase asset and increase liability

B   Increase asset and increase capital

C   Increase capital and increase liability

D   Increase capital and decrease liability

21 A business has capital of $10,000 and liabilities of $4,000.

Which of the following asset and liability figures could appear in this business' statement of financial position?

A   Assets $6,000   Liabilities $16,000

B   Assets $6,000   Liabilities $4,000

C   Assets $10,000   Liabilities $10,000

D   Assets $14,000   Liabilities $4,000

22 What is the double entry to record receipt of cash from an account receivable?

A   Debit sales   Credit receivables

B   Debit receivables   Credit cash

C   Debit cash   Credit sales

D   Debit cash   Credit receivables

23 A sole trader had opening capital of $10,000 and closing capital of $4,500. During the accounting period, the owner introduced capital of $4,000 and withdrew $8,000 for her own use.

What was her profit or loss for the accounting period?

A $9,500 loss

B $1,500 loss

C $7,500 profit

D $17,500 profit

24 **What does a debit balance usually represent?**

A   Assets and income

B   Liabilities and income

C   Assets and expenses

D   Liabilities and expenses

25 **What is the double entry required to record the purchase of a motor van on credit?**

A	Debit: motor expenses	Credit: cash
B	Debit: motor van	Credit: cash
C	Debit: motor expenses	Credit: account payable
D	Debit: motor van	Credit: account payable

26 **What is the double entry required to record the withdrawal of cash from a business bank account by the owner?**

A	Debit: drawings	Credit: cash
B	Debit: drawings	Credit: capital
C	Debit: liability	Credit: cash
D	Debit: capital	Credit: drawings

27 **What is the usual double entry to record the sale of inventory for cash?**

A	Debit: inventory account	Credit: sales account
B	Debit: cash account	Credit: sales account
C	Debit: cash account	Credit: inventory account
D	Debit: cash account	Credit: inventory account

28   A debit balance would be expected to arise when the accounts are balanced at the period end on which of the following accounts?

A   Capital

B   Sales

C   Electricity

D   Loan

29   A credit balance would be expected to arise when the accounts are balanced at the period end on which of the following accounts?

A   Drawings

B   Telephone

C   Receivables

D   Payables −

30   A business sells goods on credit to a customer who pays one month later. What are the accounting entries required to record the receipt of cash?

A   Debit: Cash at bank account   Credit: Accounts receivable

B   Debit: Cash at bank account   Credit: Accounts payable

C   Debit: Accounts receivable   Credit: Cash at bank account

D   Debit: Accounts payable   Credit: Cash at bank account

31   Which of the following describes the separate entity principle?

A   The assets of a business are a separate entity from the liabilities

B   The drawings of a business are a separate entity from the profit of the business

C   The business is a separate entity from the owner of the business

D   The owner of the business must be a separate entity from a lender to the business

32   Which of the following is a liability?

A   Trade receivables

B   Inventory

C   Bank overdraft

D   Drawings

33   Which of the following is NOT an asset?

A   Owner's capital

B   Petty cash

C   Salesman's motor car

D   Computer software

34 **Which of the following statements describes the accounting equation?**

A   Net assets = Capital − Profit − Drawings

B   Net assets = Capital − Profit + Drawings

C   Net assets = Capital + Profit + Drawings   ✓

D   Net assets = Capital + Profit − Drawings

35 **When goods are taken out of the business for personal use by the owner of a business, how will they be recorded?**

A   As drawings

B   As an expense

C   As inventory   ✓

D   As a liability

36 **If the owner of a business withdraws cash from the business bank account in order to meet her own expenses, this is classified as drawings.**

What is this an example of?

A   Internal control

B   Personal ledger accounting

C   Segregation of duties   ✓

D   The separate entity principle

37 **What is the effect upon net assets when inventory is purchased on credit?**

A   Net assets and owner's capital do not change

B   Net assets increase and owner's capital increase   ✓

C   Net assets decrease and owner's capital decreases

D   Net assets increase and owner's capital stays the same

38 **What is the effect upon net assets when an expense is paid in cash?**

A   Net assets increase and profit increases

B   Net assets decrease and profit decreases   ✓

C   Net assets remain the same and profit increases

D   Net assets remain the same and profit decreases

39   What is the nominal ledger?

A   The book where all transactions are originally recorded before being posted to ledger accounts.

Ⓑ   The book which contains a ledger account for each type of asset, liability, expense and income.   ✓

C   The book which contains all of the details of the non-current assets.

D   The book which contains all of the details of the trade receivables.

40   What is the payables ledger?

A   A record of the credit limits of each credit supplier

B   A record of the personal details of each credit supplier

Ⓒ   A record of the accounts of each credit supplier   ✓

D   A record of the accounts of each credit customer

41   Which of the following would normally be a debit balance on the ledger account?

(i)   Sales revenues (sales)

(ii)   Rent

(iii)   Drawings

(iv)   Capital

A   (i) and (iii)   ✓

Ⓑ   (ii) and (iii)

C   (i) and (iv)

D   (ii) and (iv)

42   What is a book of prime entry?

A   A ledger account where transactions are originally recorded.

Ⓑ   A record in which transactions are originally recorded before being transferred to a ledger account.   ✓

C   A separate ledger where details of a particular type of transaction are recorded in parallel to the recording in the general ledger.

D   A set of memorandum ledger accounts which back up the total figures recorded in the general ledger.

43   Which of the following is NOT a book of prime entry?

Ⓐ   Receivables ledger

B   Sales day book   ✓

C   Petty cash book

D   Transfer journal

44 Which of the following statements is true?

Ⓐ Purchase of a salesman's car is capital expenditure and repairs to a delivery van are revenue expenditure.

B Repairs to a delivery van are capital expenditure and rent for a factory is revenue expenditure. ✓

C Purchase of a salesman's car is capital expenditure and purchase of computers for office use is revenue expenditure.

D Purchase of shelving for the office is capital expenditure and purchase of computers for office use is revenue expenditure.

45 Which of the following are examples of capital expenditure?

(i) Purchase of a new computer for office use

(ii) Purchase of a second hand computer for office use

(iii) Repairs to the computer

(iv) Purchase of additional hardware to enhance the computer

A (i) only

B (i) and (iv) ✓

Ⓒ (i), (ii) and (iv)

D All four

46 Which of the following is an example of revenue expenditure?

(i) Purchase of a second hand delivery van

(ii) Purchase of stocks for resale

(iii) Repairs to the delivery van

(iv) Insurance of the delivery van

A (i), (ii) and (iii)

B (i), (ii) and (iv) ✓

Ⓒ (ii), (iii) and (iv)

D (iii) and (iv)

47 Which of the following types of expenditure would be classified as capital expenditure?

A Legal fees associated with the purchase of an office ‒

B Repairs to a delivery van

Ⓒ Rent of a leasehold property for five years

x

D Repainting the office premises

48 Which of the following types of expenditure would generally be classified as revenue expenditure?

A   Payment of tax

B   Purchase of a delivery van by a courier service

C   Extension to the office building of a toy manufacturer   ✓

(D)   Swivel chairs for resale by an office equipment retailer

49 Which of the following is an asset?

(A)   Bank deposit account

B   Bank overdraft   ✓

C   Bank loan

D   Proprietors' capital

50 Which of the following is NOT an item of capital expenditure?

(A)   Capital

B   Purchase of a new motor van

C   Purchase of a second hand factory machine   ✓

D   Replacement of the managing director's Mercedes car

51 A machinery account has a debit balance of $4,000.

What balances will occur at the end of the year to take this balance into the next period?

(A)   Dr   Machinery balance c/d   Cr   Machinery balance b/d

B   Cr   Machinery balance c/d   Dr   Machinery balance b/d –   ✗

C   Dr   Machinery balance c/d   Dr   Machinery balance b/d

D   Cr   Machinery balance c/d   Cr   Machinery balance b/d

52 A capital account has a credit balance of $40,000.

What balances will occur at the end of the year to take this balance into the next period?

(A)   Dr   Capital balance c/d   Cr   Capital balance b/d

B   Cr   Capital balance c/d   Dr   Capital balance b/d   ✓

C   Dr   Capital balance c/d   Dr   Capital balance b/d

D   Cr   Capital balance c/d   Cr   Capital balance b/d

90%

53 A business has a bank overdraft of $350 and $50 cash in hand at the end of the accounting period.

What balances will be brought down at the start of the next accounting period?

A   Dr Bank   Cr Cash

B   Cr Bank   Dr Cash   ✓

C   Dr Bank   Dr Cash

D   Cr Bank   Cr Cash

54 A business buys equipment costing $1,000 and sells equipment costing $800 in the year. The opening balance of the equipment account is $1,000.

What will be the balance CARRIED DOWN to the next accounting period?

A   Dr $800

B   Cr $800   ✓

C   Dr $1,200

D   Cr $1,200

55 A business buys machinery costing $2,000 and sells machinery costing $1,800 in the year. The opening balance of the equipment account is $2,000.

What will be the balance brought down in the next accounting period?

A   Dr $1,800

B   Cr $1,800   ?

C   Dr $2,200 —   ✗

D   Cr $2,200

56 A sole trader had opening capital of $20,000 and closing capital of $23,000. During the period, the owner introduced capital of $4,000 and withdrew $15,000 for his own use.

What was the sole trader's profit or loss during the accounting period?

A $8,000 profit

B $14,000 profit   ✓

C $15,000 profit

D $22,000 profit

57 **What does a credit entry usually represent?**

A   Assets and income

B   Liabilities and income   ✓

C   Assets and expenses

D   Liabilities and expenses

58 What is the double entry to record the purchase of plant and machinery for cash?

A Debit: plant repairs   Credit: cash

(B) Debit: plant and machinery   Credit: cash   ✓

C Debit: plant repairs   Credit: account payable

D Debit: plant and machinery   Credit: account payable

59 What is the double entry to record the introduction of capital into a business bank account by the owner?

A Debit: drawings   Credit: cash

B Debit: cash   Credit: drawings   ✓

(C) Debit: cash   Credit: capital

D Debit: capital   Credit: cash

60 A business buys goods on credit from a supplier and will pay one month later. When the payment is made, what is the double entry required to record this?

A Debit: Cash account   Credit: Accounts receivable

B Debit: Cash account   Credit: Accounts payable   ✗

(C) Debit: Accounts receivable   Credit: Cash account

D Debit: Accounts payable   Credit: Cash account

61 Which of the following a liability?

A Capital introduced

B Inventory

(C) Bank overdraft   ✓

D Drawings

62 Which of the following is NOT an asset?

A Computer equipment

B Petty cash balance

C Office photocopier   ✓

(D) Computer maintenance

63 Which of the following statements describes the accounting equation?

A Closing net assets = Opening capital − Profit − Drawings

B Closing net assets = Opening capital − Profit + Drawings   ✓

C Closing net assets = Opening capital + Profit + Drawings

(D) Closing net assets = Opening capital + Profit − Drawings

64   Which of the following are examples of capital expenditure?

(i)   Purchase of a new company car for a member of staff

(ii)   Purchase of a second-hand company car for a member of staff

(iii)   Repairs to company cars

(iv)   Cost of insuring company cars

A   (i) only

B   (i) and (ii)   ✓

C   (i), (ii) and (iv)

D   All four

65   Which of the following is an example of revenue expenditure?

(i)   Purchase of a colour printer for the office

(ii)   Purchase of paper for use in the printer

(iii)   Repairs to the printer

(iv)   Purchase of ink cartridges for the printer

A   (i), (ii) and (iii)   ✓

B   (i), (ii) and (iv)

C   (ii), (iii) and (iv)

D   (iii) and (iv)

66   Which of the following types of expenditure should be classified as capital expenditure?

A   Painting and decoration of the office

B   Purchase of a delivery van   ✓

C   Capital introduced

D   Drawings

BANKING AND PETTY CASH

67   Which of the following is the most efficient method of filing and retaining purchase invoices received from suppliers?

A   Supplier name only in alphabetical order   ✓

B   Purchase invoice date only

C   Using both supplier name in alphabetical order and purchase invoice date

D   Supplier purchase invoice number only

68 **What are the disadvantages of an organisation not having a document retention policy?**

(i)   Difficulty trying to demonstrate compliance with any legal or regulatory requirements relating to business documents

(ii)   Difficulty and wasted time trying to locate and access individual documents

(iii)   Difficulty for an organisation to raise queries with customers and/or suppliers if a discrepancy is identified

(iv)   Difficulty for an organisation to resolve queries raised by customers and/or suppliers

A   All of the above -

B   (i) (ii) and (iii) only X

C   (ii) and (iii) only

D   (i), (ii) and (iv) only

69 **Which of the following is the most efficient method of filing and retaining sales invoices?**

A   Calendar month order only

B   Sequential sales invoice number order only

C   Customer name only in alphabetical order

D   Product reference number of items sold only

70 **Why should an organisation retain completed purchase requisitions?**

A   It confirms the value of a sale to a customer by an organisation

B   It is confirmation that the goods in question were received.

C   It contains evidence of authorisation by a responsible person to confirm that there is a valid requirement or the goods/services requested

D   It is confirmation that payment was made for the goods in question

71 **What are the advantages of an organisation having a document retention policy?**

(i)   It enables an organisation to more easily locate and access documents

(ii)   It enables an organisation to review transactions and resolve queries raised by customers and/or suppliers

(iii)   It enables an organisation to review transactions and to raise queries with customers and/or suppliers if a discrepancy is identified

(iv)   It enables an organisation to meet any legal or regulatory requirements relating to retention of business documents

A   (i), (ii) and (iv) only

B   (ii) and (iii) only

C   (i), (ii) and (iii) only

D   All of the above

72 Kevin had a bank overdraft of $500 at 1 January. His only transactions during that month were the sale of goods for cash of $900 and the purchase of goods on credit for $700. At 31 January, what will be the balance on Kevin's cash at bank account?

- A $300 credit
- B $400 debit
- C $700 debit
- D $1,400 debit

73 Which of the following transactions would NOT be classified as a cash transaction?

- A Purchase of raw materials at a cost of $850, paid by cheque at the time of purchase.
- B Sale of four chairs to Mr Jones who will pay by cheque next week.
- C A transfer from the bank deposit account to the bank current account.
- D Takings placed in the shop till throughout the day.

74 Which of the following could NOT be used as a method of payment?

- A Credit card
- B Banker's draft
- C Standing order
- D Remittance advice

75 What is the title of the person who signs a cheque?

- A The drawer
- B The drawee
- C The payer
- D The payee

76 If a cheque has been signed by the payee on the reverse side, together with a written instruction to pay a third party, what is this known as:

- A An endorsement
- B A cheque guarantee
- C A crossed cheque
- D A credit transfer

77 An individual has a card issued by his bank that allows him to make purchases up to a certain credit limit. He receives a statement each month detailing his purchases and he is required to pay off the total amount of the balance outstanding each month.

What is this an example of?

A   A debit card

B   A credit card

C   A charge card

D   A cheque guarantee card

78 Each month the amount of money that you owe on a store credit card is paid automatically and directly to the store out of your bank account. The amount and the precise date of payment will vary each month.

What is this an example of?

A   A standing order

B   A credit transfer

C   A mail transfer

D   A direct debit

79 **Who is the drawee of a cheque?**

A   The person or business who is paying

B   The person or business who is being paid

C   The person who signs the cheque

D   The bank of the person or business who is paying

80 **If two parallel vertical lines are drawn on the face of a cheque, what does this mean?**

A   Only the payee can cash the cheque at the bank.

B   This cheque can only be deposited in the payee's bank account.

C   This cheque cannot be cashed at the bank, it can only be paid into a bank account.

D   This is now a bearer cheque which is payable to the holder.

81 There is a card which can be used to pay for goods, the amount of which is electronically deducted from your bank balance immediately.

What type of card is this?

A   A debit card

B   A credit card

C   A cheque guarantee card

D   A charge card

82 Goldie makes regular quarterly payments for gas and electricity. Goldie completed a form of authorisation and the suppliers then set up their own arrangement with the bank to collect amounts due. Goldie is always informed of these amounts in advance.

What is this method of payment?

A A direct debit

B An inter-bank transfer

C A standing order

D EFTPOS

83 **What is the title of a note that accompanies a cheque payment to a supplier, detailing the invoices being paid?**

A A supplier's statement

B A debit note

C A remittance advice

D A remittance list

84 Martin pays monthly bill for heat and light charges by instructing his bank to make a monthly payment from his current account in favour of the power supply company. As Martin's power usage will change each month, Martin's authorisation to the bank does not require him to issue a new instruction to his bank to pay the revised amount to the power company.

What method of payment is Martin using?

A Crossed cheque

B Direct debit

C Standing order

D Payable order

85 **Who is the drawer of a cheque?**

A The recipient of the cheque who has received the cheque as a form of payment

B The account holder whose account will be debited when the cheque is presented

C The bank and branch upon which the cheque is drawn

D The bank and branch through which the cheque is presented for payment

86 **What card will normally be requested to accompany a payment by cheque?**

A Credit card

B Cheque guarantee card

C Mastercard

D Store card

87 What information/details on a credit card should a cashier check when they receive a payment for goods?

(i)   It is signed

(ii)   It is valid at that day's date

(iii)   It has not been altered/tampered with

(iv)   It is issued by a bank

A   All

B   (i), (ii) and (iii) only

C   (i) and (ii) only

D   (ii) and (iv) only

88 What is the normal period of time required for a cheque to be cleared between banks using the UK clearing system?

A   7 working days

B   5 working days

C   10 working days

D   3 working days

89 Which of the following constitute a contractual relationship between a bank and its customers?

(i)   Receivable/Payable

(ii)   Principal/Agent

(iii)   Mortgagor/Mortgagee

(iv)   Bailor/Bailee

A   All

B   (i) and (iv) only

C   (i) and (ii) only

D   (i), (ii) and (iii) only

90 A petty cash system operates on a $120 imprest system. At the end of a month there is $67.23 of valid petty cash vouchers in the petty cash box. How much cash should be taken out of the bank account in order to restore it to the correct amount?

A $52.77 –

B $67.23

C $120.00

D $187.23

91 **Which of the following are duties of the customer towards their bank?**

(i)   Promote the bank's services

(ii)   Not encourage fraudulent activities

(iii)   Not to misuse any cheque guarantee card

(iv)   Not to open an account elsewhere without notice

A   All

B   (i), (ii) and (iv) only

C   (ii) and (iii) only

D   (i), (ii) and (iii) only

92 On a particular day, the cash register in a shop shows that cash sales were made of $1,073.21. The cash in the till at the end of the day totalled $1,318.76 and a cash float of $250 is always carried in the till.

Which of the following would NOT be a valid reason for the difference between the cash in the till and the cash register records?

A   All of the cash received was not paid into the till

B   A customer was given too much change

C   The price for goods entered into the cash register was higher than that charged to the customer

D   The price for goods entered into the cash register was lower than that charged to the customer

93 **What should happen to a cheque on which F Jones is the drawer and A Smith is the payee and which also contains the crossing "Account payee"?**

A   It can be paid out in cash when presented at the bank

B   It must be paid into a bank account, although there is no restriction on which bank account it is paid into

C   It must be paid into a bank account in the name of A Smith

D   It must be paid into a bank account in the name of F Jones

94 A cash advance of $20 is taken out of the petty cash box by an employee for refreshments for a client and an authorised voucher for $20 put into the petty cash box. The employee only spends $17.65 on refreshments.

What is the petty cash procedure required?

A   The employee keeps the change of $2.35

B   The employee keeps the change of $2.35 and the petty cash voucher is altered to read $17.65

C   The employee returns the $2.35

D   The employee returns the $2.35 and the petty cash voucher is altered to read $17.65

95   Which of the following documents would be required when paying in the daily takings to the bank?

(i)   Cheques received

(ii)   Copy credit card vouchers

(iii)   Cheque remittance list

(iv)   Copy credit card summary

A   (i) and (ii) only

B   (i), (ii) and (iv) only

C   (i), (iii) and (iv) only

D   All four

96   A petty cash system is run on an imprest system of $100. At the end of March the cash in the petty cash box totalled $36.58 and the vouchers totalled $53.42.

Which of the following would NOT be a valid reason for the difference?

A   Money had been taken out of the petty cash box without an authorised voucher to support it.

B   The incorrect amount of cash had been paid out of the petty cash box in for an authorised voucher.

C   A petty cash voucher had been made out for the wrong amount but the amount of cash paid out agreed with the voucher.

D   A petty cash voucher had been made out for the wrong amount but the correct amount of cash had been paid out.

97   Henry is preparing a bank paying-in slip at the end of the day in his shop. His till roll shows sales of $193.24. Henry always maintains a float of $25 in the till and takes $20 each day as his wages.

How much will Henry pay into the bank today?

A $213.24

B $193.24

C $173.24

D $148.24

98   For which of the following payments would petty cash NOT normally be used?

A $9.50 for cleaning the shop windows

B $26.00 for coffee and tea for office staff

C $125.00 invoice for postage via a courier

D $37.00 train fare to a business conference

99 At the beginning of March, the petty cash tin contained a float of $65. During the month, petty cash payments totalled $64 and a cheque for $50 was cashed at the bank to replenish the float.

What was the petty cash float at the beginning of April?

A $1

B $51

C $75

D $80

100 **Where should the petty cash tin be kept?**

A   In a drawer

B   On the desk

C   In a safe

D   On a cabinet

101 **What is the purpose of petty cash?**

A   To act as a cash float

B   To cover all out of pocket expenses

C   To pay small and/or irregular amounts

D   To finance the office parties

102 **How can you ensure that petty cash payments have been made for authentic expenditure?**

A   By recording the vouchers immediately in the petty cash book

B   By ensuring the petty cash vouchers are signed

C   By stapling appropriate receipts to the vouchers

D   Allowing only certain employees to have access to petty cash

103 **In January a business receives a cheque dated January of the previous year. What should they do with this cheque?**

A   Pay it into the bank

B   Alter the date

C   Write 'refer to drawer' on the cheque

D   Return it to the customer for alteration

104 **Which form of payment commonly uses BACS?**

    A   Cheque

    B   Credit card

    C   Debit card

    (D)   Payroll

105 **What information is disclosed on a bank statement?**

    (A)   The transactions passing through the bank account of a business

    B   The transactions between customer and supplier

    C   Petty cash transactions

    D   Transactions on a company credit card

106 When presenting a debit card to pay for goods at a supermarket checkout, the card is rejected with the message that the limit has been exceeded.

    What action should the checkout operator take?

    (A)   Ask the customer to make payment by some other means

    B   Authorise an increased debit card limit for the customer

    C   Call the police and have the customer arrested

    D   Let the customer take the goods and come back later to make payment

107 **Which of the following is a valid method of payment?**

    A   A credit card in excess of its limit

    B   A cheque on which the amounts in words and figures differ

    (C)   Cash

    D   Barter

108 **What is needed for a cheque to be properly authorised?**

    A   Sufficient money in the bank

    (B)   Evidence of an underlying transaction and an approved requisition

    C   A receipt stapled to an invoice

    D   A remittance advice and the accompanying statement from supplier

109 **A cheque is automatically printed by a computerised accounting system for payment to be made to the supplier. How does this benefit the business?**

    A   It prevents fraud

    (B)   There are unlikely to be technical mistakes on the cheque

    C   The cheque does not require authorisation

    D   It saves the need to check and sign the cheque

110 Why would tills be checked from time to time by managers and other responsible staff who are NOT usually involved in the receipt and payment of cash?

    A   To enable the managers and others to handle cash

    (B)   As a security measure to check the work of cashiers

    C   To assess the sales performance of the organisation

    D   As a way of ensuring documentation is being dealt with correctly

111 What is the double entry to record the reimbursement of the petty cash float?

    (A)   Debit: petty cash   Credit: cash

    B   Debit: expenses   Credit: cash

    C   Debit: cash   Credit: petty cash

    D   Debit: cash   Credit: expenses

112 DBB Co accounts for petty cash using the imprest system. The following is a summary of DBB Co's petty cash transactions for the week ended 29 August 20X6:

Income	$	Expenditure	$
Opening balance	100	Travelling expenses	54
Sale of stationery	35	Office refreshments	36
Sale of vending machine tokens	20	Cleaning materials	17

What sum should be reclaimed by the accounts assistant at the end of the week?

    A $100

    B $107   54+36+17 -35-20

    C $48

    (D) $52

113 During the week ended 27 January 20X8, ARK Co acquired significant petty cash receipts when cash takings from office vending machines were emptied. As the petty cash balance is now more than enough to meet normal petty cash requirements, some of the surplus cash will be paid into the bank account.

What is the double entry required to record the payment of petty cash into the bank account?

    A   Debit: Petty cash   Credit: Bank

    B   Debit: Expenses   Credit: Bank

    (C)   Debit: Bank   Credit: Petty cash

    D   Debit: Expenses   Credit: Petty cash

SALES AND SALES RETURNS

114   A Co sold goods to the value of $500 (net) to Harper.

In A Co's accounting records, what would be the debit to Harper's account if sales tax is payable at the rate of 17.5%?

A $412.50

B $500.00

C $587.50

D $606.06

(handwritten: (500 × 17.5) / 100 = ANS   ANS + 500)

115   A summary of the transactions of Ramsgate, who is registered for sales tax at 17.5%, shows the following for the month of August 20X9.

Outputs $60,000 (exclusive of sales tax) *10 500*

Inputs $40,286 (inclusive of sales tax)

At the beginning of the period Ramsgate owed $3,400 to the taxation authorities, and during the period he has paid $2,600 to them.

At the end of the accounting period, what is the amount due to the taxation authorities?

A $3,700

B $3,930

C $4,400

D $5,300

(handwritten sales tax account:
Sales tax account
Payables 6,000 | Balance b/d 3,400
Bank 2,600 | Receivables 10,500
Balance c/d 5,300
13,900 | 13,900
Balance b/d 5,300)

116   **In which book of prime entry would the sales tax on credit sales be recorded?**

A   Sales day book

B   Purchases day book

C   Cash receipts book

D   Cash payments book

117   **In which books of prime entry would the following transactions be entered?**

A credit sale for $387 and a cash sale of $200.

A   The cash book and sales day book

B   The petty cash book and sales day book

C   The purchase day book and sales day book

D   The journal and cash book

118 **Which of the following statements is true in relation to the sales account?**

A   It is credited with the total of sales made, including sales tax

(B) It is credited with the total of sales made, excluding sales tax

C   It is debited with the total of sales made, including sales tax

D   It is debited with the total of sales made, excluding sales tax

119 **In which book of prime entry would the sales tax on cash sales be recorded?**

A   Sales day book

B   Purchases day book

(C) Cash book

D   Journal

120 A business sold goods that had a net value of $600 to Lucid plc.

What entries are required to record this transaction if sales tax is payable at 17.5%?

A   Dr Lucid plc $600, Dr sales tax $105, Cr Sales $705

(B) Dr Lucid plc $705, Cr sales tax $105, Cr Sales $600

C   Dr Lucid plc $600, Cr sales tax $105, Cr Sales $600

D   Dr Sales $600, Dr sales tax $105, Cr Lucid plc $705

121 A sales tax registered business issued a sales invoice for goods with a list price of $1,325.00 on which a trade discount of 20% was given. The goods were rated for sales tax at 10%.

What was the sales tax charged on the invoice?

(A) $106.00

B $132.50

C $238.50

D $119.25

$1,325 \times 0.80 = {}^1ANS$

${}^1ANS \times 0.9 = {}^2ANS$

${}^1ANS - {}^2ANS$

122 Scott is preparing an invoice for the sales of a machine. The list price of the machine is $12,000, which is subject to a trade discount of 10%. The sale is subject to sales tax at 15%.

How much sales tax should be included in the invoice?

A $1,530

(B) $1,620

C $1,080

D $1.020

$12,000 \times 90\% \times 15\% = 1,620$

$\frac{90}{100} \times 12,000 = 10,800$

$\frac{15}{100} \times 10800 = 1,620$

123 Which of the following transactions is a credit transaction?

    A   Sale of goods for cash

    B   Sale of goods and receipt of a cheque

    (C)   Sale of goods with payment due in 60 days

    D   Receipt of a cheque for goods sold 40 days ago

124 Megan was invoiced for $100 less 5% trade discount. Megan's supplier is not registered for sales tax.

When Megan pays the invoice, how much will she pay?

    A $92.50

    B $92.63 $100 \times 95\% = 95.00$

    (C) $95.00

    D $7.50

125 A sale is made for $414 inclusive of sales tax at 15%. What is the entry to the sales account?

    A   Debit $360

    (B)   Credit $360

    C   Debit $414

    D   Credit $414

126 Cash of $282 was received from a receivable that had purchased goods on credit for $240 plus sales tax at 17.5%.

What is the double entry required to record this receipt?

A	Debit cash $282	Credit sales $240
		Credit sales tax $42
B	Debit cash $282	Credit sales $282
C	Debit cash $282	Credit receivables $240
		Credit sales tax $42
(D)	Debit cash $282	Credit receivables $282

127 What does a debit balance on the sales tax account represent?

    A   An amount of sales tax owing to the tax authorities

    B   A sales tax expense to be written off in the profit and loss account

    (C)   An amount of sales tax due from the tax authorities

    D   Sales tax income to be included in the statement of comprehensive income

128 At the start of a month, accounts receivable owed $4,529. During the month total sales were $16,540 of which 40% were for cash. Cash was received from receivables of $7,231 during the month.

What was the balance of accounts receivable at the end of the month?

 A $1,836

 B $3,914

 C $5,144

 (D) $7,222

Handwritten working:
Accounts Receivable
opening bal 4,524 | cash 7,231
sales 16,540 × 60% | Balance c/d 7,222
9,924
= 14,453 | = 14,453

129 During a three-month period, a business made sales of $69,200 plus sales tax at 15%. The balance on the receivables account at the start of the period was $5,329 and at the end of the period $4,771.

How much cash was received from receivables during the period?

 A $68,642

 B $69,758

 C $79,022

 (D) $80,138

Handwritten working:
Receivables Account
opening 5,329 | cash bal 80,138
sales (69200 × 1.15) | closing bal 4,771
84,904 | 84,904

130 Avalon gives his customers individual trade discounts from the list price and a general 5% cash discount for early settlement of invoices within 7 days of issue. A new customer, Nolava negotiates a 25% trade discount. As Nolava is a new customer, it is not expected to take advantage of the early settlement discount terms. Nolava's transactions during June were as follows:

June 12	Buys goods with a $5,000 list price
June 15	Returns goods with a $1,000 list price as faulty
June 16	Pays half of the net balance on his account

How much does Nolava owe Avalon at the end of June?

 A $1,425

 (B) $1,500

 C $2,000

 D $2,850

131 If a credit customer takes advantage of early settlement discount terms, when they were NOT originally expected to do so, how would the settlement discount be accounted for?

 A It would increase expenses

 (B) It would be a reduction in revenue receivable

 C It would be offset against discount received

 D It would increase cost of sales

132 Victoria sells materials to Fraser for $240. Fraser manufactures goods from these materials and sells them to a customer, Helen, for $360 plus sales tax. Victoria and Fraser are sales tax registered traders and the goods rate of sales tax is 17.5%.

How much sales tax is paid to the taxation authorities by each party to the transactions?

A	Victoria pays	$42 and Fraser pays	$63	
B	Fraser pays	$42 and Helen pays	$63	
(C)	Victoria pays	$42 and Fraser pays	$21	
D	Fraser pays	$42 and Helen pays	$21	

133 A business has an opening balance on the sales tax account showing an amount owing to the taxation authorities of $3,210. During the period there were sales of $21,700, excluding sales tax, and purchases of $18,480, including sales tax. During the period $2,890 was paid to the taxation authorities. The standard rate of sales tax is 10%.

What is the balance carried forward on the sales tax account at the end of the period?

A $642 credit

(B) $810 credit

C $1,042 credit

D $196 credit

134 Which of the following procedures should help to reduce overdue receivables' balances?

(A) Improved debt collection methods

B An increase in the bank overdraft facility

C Credit customers paying invoices more slowly

D An increase in credit facilities to customers

135 Charles sold goods for $1,200 and bought goods for $810. Both transactions included sales tax at 20% in the prices given.

How much will Charles pay to the tax authorities in respect of these two transactions?

A $38.00

(B) $65.00

C $78.00

D $390.00

136 Which of the following statements best explains what output tax is?

A It is a sales tax on purchases

(B) It is a sales tax on sales

C It is a payment to the tax authorities

D It is a repayment from the tax authorities

137 On 1 February the credit balance on Josh's Sales tax account was $2,400. During the month, sales tax on sales was $1,050, sales tax on purchases and other expenses was $900 and a repayment of sales tax was received of $200.

What was the credit balance on the sales tax account at 28 February?

A $2,050

B $2,350

C $2,450

(D) $2,750

138 Who normally suffers the burden of sales tax?

A   The first supplier in the chain of supply

B   The manufacturer

C   The retailer

(D) The consumer

139 During a month a business made sales of $24,600 and purchases of $15,200 exclusive of sales tax. The business is registered for sales tax and both sales and purchases are subject to sales tax at 17.5%.

What is the balance on the sales tax account at the end of the month if the opening balance was zero?

A   A debit balance of $1,645

(B) A credit balance of $1,645

C   A debit balance of $11,045

D   A credit balance of $11,045

140 During a three-month period a business made the following sales and purchases:

Sales $34,800 (exclusive of sales tax at 17.5%)

Purchases $30,785 (inclusive of sales tax at 17.5%)

What is the balance on the sales tax account at the end of the three-month period if the opening balance was zero?

A $598

B $703

(C) $1,505

D $8,600

141 During a three-month period a business made sales of $72,145, including sales tax at 17.5%, and purchases of $54,200, excluding sales tax at 17.5%. There was an amount due to the taxation authorities at 17.5% at the start of the three-month period totalling $1,354.

What was the balance on the sales tax account at the end of the three-month period?

A $94

B $1,260

C $2,614

D $4,669

Sales tax account

Input sales tax 9485 | Opening balance 1,354
(54,200 x 0.175) | Output sales tax 10,745
Balance c/d 2614 | (72,145 x 17.5/117.5)
12,099 | 12,099

142 At what point should sales tax on a credit sale be recorded?

A   By the supplier when the invoice is issued and by the customer when the invoice is received

B   By the supplier when the invoice is issued and by the customer when the payment is made to the supplier

C   By the supplier when the cash payment is received and by the customer when the invoice is received

D   By the supplier when the cash payment is received and by the customer when the cash payment is made

143 When must a business charge sales tax on its sales?

A   If it is a limited liability entity

B   If it sells goods and services

C   If it is registered to account for sales tax

D   If it has been trading for more than one year

144 Which of the following would be appropriate to be written off as an irrecoverable debt?

A   A cash sale

B   A credit sale made within the last month

C   A credit sale over the organisation's credit limit made in the last week

D   A credit sale within the organisation's credit limit and outstanding for a year

145 Where is a credit note first recorded in a manual book-keeping system?

A   In an aged receivables' analysis

B   In a sales day book

C   In a sales returns day book

D   In the receivables ledger

146 **What is the purpose of an aged receivables' analysis?**

(A) To monitor the time receivables are outstanding

B To list irrecoverable debts

C To hold receivables temporarily

D To calculate credit limits

147 **What is the purpose of coding in a computerised accounting system?**

A It authorises transactions

(B) It identifies appropriate accounts for posting

C It records credit limits for accounts receivable

D It transfers ledger balances automatically

148 **Which of the following entries is used to record an irrecoverable debt?**

A Dr Account receivable   Cr Irrecoverable debts

(B) Dr Irrecoverable debts   Cr Account receivable

C Dr Profit and loss account   Cr Irrecoverable debts

D Dr Irrecoverable debts   Cr Profit and loss account

149 **Why would you NOT send a statement to an account written off as an irrecoverable debt?**

(A) Doing so would advise the receivable there is no need to pay

B Doing so would encourage the receivable to pay

C It is against the law of contract to do so

D It is against data protection legislation to do so

150 An account receivable is for $800. The customer is experiencing severe difficulties and has agreed to return goods which it had purchased for $600. The supplier decides to write off the remaining amount.

What is the double entry required by the supplier to record this?

A Dr Account receivable $800; Cr Sales returns $600; Cr Irrecoverable debts $200

B Dr Irrecoverable debts $200; Dr Bank $600; Cr Sales returns $800

(C) Dr Irrecoverable debts $200; Dr Sales returns $600; Cr Account receivable $800

D Dr Sales returns $800; Cr Irrecoverable debt $200; Cr Bank $600

151 A business sold goods to the value of $500 (net) to Smart.

What would be the debit to receivables if sales tax is payable at a rate of 20%?

A $416.67

B $500.00

C $583.33

(D) $600.00

152 A summary of the transactions of Sandstone, who is registered for sales tax at 20%, showed the following for the month of May 20X5.

Outputs $80,000 (exclusive of sales tax) *Purchases*

Inputs $64,200 (inclusive of sales tax) *Sales*

At the beginning of the period Sandstone owed $4.500 to the taxation authorities, and during the period he paid $3,600 to the taxation authorities.

At the end of the period, how much is owing to the taxation authorities?

A $2,800

B $4,400

(C) $6,200

D $13,400

Sales tax account

Input tax 10700 | Opening balance 4,500
Cash paid 3,600 | Output tax (80,000 × 0.2) 16000
Balance c/d 6,200 |
20500   20500

153 A sales tax registered business issued a sales invoice for goods with a list price of $1,480.00. A trade discount of 5% was given. The goods were rated for sales tax at 20%.

What was the gross value of the invoice?

A $1,420.80

(B) $1,687.20

C $1,776.00

D $1,476.30

154 Farmer is preparing an invoice for the sale of a machine. The list price of the machine is $10,500, on which a trade discount of 8% will be made. The sale is subject to sales tax at 20%.

What will be the gross value of the invoice?

A $9,072.00

B $10,080.00

C $10,432.80

(D) $11,592.00

$\frac{10500}{1} \times \frac{20}{100} = \frac{210,000}{100}$

$12,600 \times 0.08 = 11,592$

155 Celine makes a sale on credit for $423 excluding sales tax at 20%.

What is the entry to the trade receivables account?

A Debit $423.00

B Credit $507.60

(C) Debit $507.60

D Credit $423.00

$423 \times 1.2 = 507.60$

156 In which book of prime entry would the sales tax on a cash sale be recorded?

A   Sales day book

B   Purchases day book

Ⓒ   Cash receipts book

D   Cash payments book

157 MAR Co is preparing an invoice for the sale of one of its products. The list price of the product is $14,500, on which a trade discount of 4% was granted. MAR Co has also offered the customer early settlement discount of 5% if payment is made within 14 days. The customer is expected to take up the offer of early settlement discount and pay within 14 days. The sales invoice was prepared on that basis.

What was the gross value of the invoice?

A $13,920.00

B $13,775.00

C $14,500.00

Ⓓ $13,224.00

14500 × 0.04 = 580   14500 − 580 = 13920

13920 × 0.05 = 696   13920 − 696 = 13224

PURCHASES AND PURCHASE RETURNS

158 Janice buys a dress costing $120, shoes costing $60 and a jacket costing $190. These are all gross figures, inclusive of sales tax at 17.5%.

How much sales tax in total has Janice paid?

Ⓐ $55.11

B $64.75

C $74.48

D $68.51

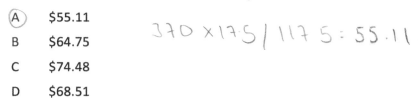

370 × 17.5 / 117.5 = 55.11

159 Which of the following is the correct posting from the purchase day book?

Ⓐ   Dr General ledger purchase account, Cr Suppliers' accounts in payables ledger

B   Dr General ledger purchase account, Cr Cash book

C   Dr Suppliers' accounts in payables ledger, Cr General ledger purchase account

D   Dr Cash book, Cr General ledger purchase account

160 WHE returned goods that had a net value of $800 to Rawlins Ltd. In WHE's accounting records, what would be the value of the debit made in Rawlins Ltd's payables ledger account if sales tax is payable at the rate of 17.5%?

A $660.00

B $800.00

Ⓒ $940.00

D $969.70

$800 \times 0.175 = 140$

$800 + 140 = 940$

161 WRE is registered for sales tax and purchased goods that had a net value of $700 plus sales tax on credit from Roper.

What would be the value of the debit to WRE's purchases account if sales tax is payable at the rate of 17.5%?

A $577.50

Ⓑ $700.00

C $822.50

D $848.48

162 Rivano has a balance of $350,000 on its payables ledger control account at 31 May 20X4.

What does this balance indicate?

A It has bought $350,000 of goods in May

B It is owed $350,000 by its customers

Ⓒ It owes $350,000 to its suppliers

D It has paid $350,000 to its suppliers in May

163 A trader who is not registered for sales tax purposes buys goods on credit. These goods have a list price of $2,000 and the trader is granted a trade discount of 20%. The goods are subject to sales tax at 17.5%.

What amount should be used to record this purchase when the purchases account is debited and the supplier's account is credited?

A $1,600

Ⓑ $1,880

C $2,000

D $2,350

$2000 \times 1.2 = 2400$ $2400 - 2000 = 400$

$1600 \times 0.175 = 280$ $1600 + 280 = 1880$

164 A business had sales (including sales tax) of $45,237.50, and purchases (excluding sales tax) of $31,500.00. There was a nil balance on the sales tax account at start of the accounting period.

What was the closing balance on the sales tax account, assuming all items are subject to sales tax at 10%?

A $962.50 credit

B $1,058.75 credit

C $1,248.86 credit

D $1,373.75 credit

Handwritten annotations:
$45,237.50 \times 10/110 = 4,112.50$
$31,500 \times 0.10 = 3,150 = 962.50$
$4,112.50 - 3,150 = 962.50$

165 Goods were returned by Ryan to his supplier that had a net value of $200.

What accounting entries should Ryan make to record this transaction if sales tax is payable at 15%?

A   Dr Payables ledger control account $230, Cr Sales tax $30, Cr Returns outwards $200

B   Dr Returns outwards $200, Dr Sales tax $30, Cr Payables ledger control account $230

C   Dr Purchases $200, Dr Sales tax $30, Cr Payables ledger control account $230

D   Dr Payables ledger control account $230, Cr Sales tax $200, Cr Returns outwards $30

166 What is the effect of payment of cash to an account payable?

A   It will increase accounts receivable and reduce cash balance

B   It will reduce cash balance and reduce current liabilities

C   It will reduce accounts payable and increase purchases

D   It will increase accounts payable and reduce cash balance

167 What the accounting entries are required to record goods returned outwards?

A   Credit purchases account and debit customer's account

B   Credit returns outwards account and debit customer's account

C   Credit returns outwards account and debit payables account

D   Credit payables account and debit returns outwards account

168 Anthony receives goods from Brad on credit terms and Anthony subsequently pays by cheque. Anthony then discovers that the goods are faulty and cancels the cheque after it is issued but before it is cashed by Brad.

How should Anthony record the cancellation of the cheque in his books?

A   Debit payables   Credit returns outwards

B   Credit bank   Debit payables

C   Debit bank   Credit returns outwards

D   Credit payables   Debit returns outwards

169 Which is of the following is the logical order in which the given documents would appear in a business system?

    A   Purchase requisition, delivery note, purchase order, goods received note

    B   Purchase order, delivery note, purchase requisition, goods received note

    (C)   Purchase requisition, purchase order, delivery note, goods received note

    D   Purchase requisition, purchase order, goods received note, delivery note

170 Which of the following is NOT a feature or purpose of a purchase invoice?

    A   To record the amount of the sales tax on the purchase

    (B)   To post the sales tax to the purchases returns day book

    C   To state the date that payment is due

    D   To record the amount and type of goods that were purchased

171 Which of the following details would be inappropriate on a purchase order issued by one company to another, both of which are registered for sales tax purposes?

    A   Registered office and company registration number

    B   Sales tax registration number

    C   Quantity and price of goods ordered

    (D)   Sales tax on goods ordered *At the time of sale.*

172 What is the double entry required to record a purchase on credit?

    A   Debit purchases   Credit receivables

    B   Debit inventory   Credit payables

    C   Debit payables   Credit purchases

    (D)   Debit purchases   Credit payables

173 If an invoice states that the settlement terms are 'net 30 days', what does it indicate?

    A   That the invoice amount, net of sales tax, is payable 30 days from receipt of the goods

    B   That the invoice amount, net of sales tax, is payable 30 days from the invoice date

    C   That the invoice amount, gross of sales tax, is payable 30 days from receipt of the goods

    (D)   That the invoice amount, gross of sales tax, is payable 30 days from the invoice date

174 The closing balance on the trade payables account for a period was $3,528. During the period cash paid to payables was $11,583. The opening balance on the trade payables account was $2,660.

What were the credit purchases for the period?

A $10,715

B $11,798

C $12,451

D $13,534

175 The following information is available about a business:

Opening payables	$14,550
Closing payables	$12,560
Payments for purchases in the period	$85,460

Of the payments for purchases, $35,640 was for cash purchases.

What was the amount of purchases on credit for the period?

A $47,830

B $48,810

C $49,820

D $83,470

176 A business had accounts payable at the end of its accounting period of $6,538 and had made purchases during the period totalling $85,400 of which 46% were for cash. The balance on the accounts payable account at the start of the period had been $6,711.

How much cash was paid to trade payables during the period?

A $39,284

B $39,457

C $45,943

D $46,289

177 A business which is registered for sales tax had a closing balance on its trade payables account of $4,286. During the period purchases on credit of $25,640 excluding sales tax at 17.5% were made and payments to payables totalled $29,660.

What was the balance at the start of the period on the trade payables account?

A $266

B $3,819

C $4,753

D $8,306

178 Which of the following accounts would NOT appear in the general ledger?

A   Motor vehicles

B   Motor repairs

C   Settlement discounts received

(D)   Trade discounts

179 What is the double entry required to record a discount received?

A   Debit: Discounts received   Credit: Accounts receivable

B   Debit: Accounts receivable   Credit: Discounts received

C   Debit: Discounts received   Credit: Accounts payable

(D)   Debit: Accounts payable   Credit: Discounts received

180 Premier Co sold goods on credit to Carling Co with the offer of a settlement discount. Carling Co does not normally take advantage of settlement discount terms. However, on this occasion, Carling does pay early and is entitled to early settlement discount.

How would the settlement of the sales invoice be recorded in Premier Co's books?

A	Debit	Cash	Credit	Carling Co
	Debit	Discount received		
B	Debit	Cash	Credit	Discount received
			Credit	Carling Co
(C)	Debit	Cash	Credit	Carling Co
	Debit	Revenue		
D	Debit	Cash	Credit	Revenue
			Credit	Carling Co

181 Premier Co sold goods on credit to Maycee Co with the offer of a settlement discount. Maycee Co does pay early and is entitled to the settlement discount. How would the settlement of this invoice be recorded in Maycee Co's accounting records?

A	Debit	Premier Co	Credit	Cash
	Debit	Discount received		
(B)	Debit	Premier Co	Credit	Discount received
			Credit	Cash
C	Debit	Premier Co	Credit	Cash
	Debit	Revenue		
D	Debit	Premier Co	Credit	Revenue
			Credit	Cash

182 Marsh Co is a supplier (code number 2016). Kyle purchased (purchases code 4000) goods costing $540 plus $94.50 sales tax (sales tax code 1034) from Marsh Co.

How will this be coded and posted In Kyle's computerised ledgers?

A   Dr 2016; Dr 4000; Cr 1034

B   Dr 2016; Cr 4000; Cr 1034

C   Dr 4000; Dr 1034; Cr 2016

D   Dr 4000; Cr 1034; Cr 2016

183 **Which of the following is a good reason to maintain an aged payables analysis?**

A   To detect potential irrecoverable debts

B   To prevent the business missing opportunities to claim discounts

C   To provide a list of accounts payable outstanding

D   To identify orders which have not yet been delivered

184 **Which of the following would be identified by matching a supplier statement against the transactions within the month?**

A   Incorrect calculations on invoices

B   Non-delivery of goods charged

C   Incorrect trade discounts

D   Duplication of invoices

185 A business offers internet ordering and payment facilities. A customer purchases goods for $200 plus sales tax at 17.5% by credit card.

How would this transaction be posted to the accounts of the buyer?

A   Dr Bank $200; Dr Sales tax $35; Cr Purchases $235

B   Dr Purchases $200; Dr Sales tax $35; Cr: Account payable

C   Dr Purchases $200; Dr Sales tax $35; Cr Credit card account $235

D   Dr Account payable $235; Cr Credit card account $235

186 **What will be the effect on a business if a number of transactions are coded incorrectly and posted within the computerised accounting system?**

A   The accounts will not be representative of the assets, liabilities, income and expenses

B   The accounts will not balance

C   The sales and purchases will be mixed up and suppliers' and customers' accounts will be misleading

D   The business would be acting illegally

187 **For a business registered to account for sales tax, what entries are made in the purchases account?**

A   It is credited with the total of purchases made, including sales tax

B   It is credited with the total of purchases made, excluding sales tax

C   It is debited with the total of purchases made, including sales tax

D   It is debited with the total of purchases made, excluding sales tax

188 **For a business registered to account for sales tax, what entries are made in the sales tax account?**

A   It is credited with cash paid to the tax authorities

B   It is debited with sales tax on sales

C   It is debited with sales tax on purchases

D   It is credited with sales tax on purchases

189 **Carter purchased goods from Miller that were identified as faulty. What is the double entry in Carter's accounting records to account for the return of these goods?**

A   Debit: purchase returns   Credit: accounts payable

B   Debit: accounts payable   Credit: purchase returns

C   Debit: sales returns   Credit: accounts payable

D   Debit: accounts payable   Credit: sales returns

190 Mylee purchased goods for $800 less 5% trade discount and which was eligible for a settlement discount of 3.5% if paid within ten days. Mylee's supplier is not registered for sales tax.

If Mylee pays the invoice to take advantage of the settlement discount, how much will she pay?

A $733.40

B $800.00

C $772.00

D $786.60

191 **In which book of prime entry would the sales tax on cash a purchase be recorded?**

A   Sales day book

B   Purchases day book

C   Cash receipts book

D   Cash payments book

PAYROLL

192   Seb packs goods on an assembly line. He is paid a different amount each week, depending on his output of assembled goods.

By what method of remuneration is Seb paid?

(A)   Piecework

B   Commission

C   Hourly paid

D   Salaried

193   For the month of May, the following figures have been extracted from a trader's records with regard to wages.

(i)   Employees' social security $678

(ii)   Gross basic wages $9,900

(iii)   Income tax $2,000

(iv)   Employer's social security $925

What will be the total charge for wages and salaries in the final accounts?

(A) $10,825

B $10,578

C $11,503

D $13,503

194   John and Mike are both paid by piecework. The terms of their employment are:

(i)   John is paid $1.15 for each unit he produces with a weekly minimum wage of $165.00.

(ii)   Mike is paid $1.10 per unit for each of the first 140 units he produces, $1.15 per unit for the next 20 units produced and $1.20 per unit for any additional units.

In a given week John produced 135 units and Mike produced 175 units.

What was the gross pay for each employee for the week?

	John	Mike
A	$155.25	$195.00
B	$155.25	$210.00
C	$165.00	$195.00
D	$165.00	$210.00

JOHN = 1.15 × 135 = 155.25 MIN 165

MIKE = 1.10 × 140 = 154

1.15 × 20 = 23

1.20 × 15 = 18

= 195

195   What is the purpose of an income tax code?

A   To determine the personal allowances available to an employee

B   To determine the amount of employee's social security that must be deducted

C   To determine the amount of employer's social security that must be paid

(D)   To reflect the tax allowances and reliefs available to an employee

196   James and Jake are both hourly paid employees. Their employment conditions are as follows:

(i)   James works a basic 40-hour week at an hourly rate of $6.20. Overtime is paid at the rate of time and half for week days and double time for weekends.

(ii)   Jake works a basic 35-hour week at an hourly rate of $7.40. Overtime is paid at a rate of time and half for the first 6 hours and double time thereafter.

During a week James and Jake both worked for 48 hours, 3 of which were at the weekend.

What is the gross pay for each employee for that week?

	James	Jake
A	$331.70	$392.20
(B)	$331.70	$429.20
C	$381.30	$392.20
D	$381.30	$429.20

Handwritten working:
James = 40 × 6.20 = 248
5 × 9.3 = 46.5
3 × 12.4 = 37.2
= 331.70

Jake = 35 × 7.40 = 259
6 × 11.1 = 66.6
7 × 14.8 = 103.6
= 429.60

197   Percy and Peter work for an organisation that has a bonus scheme which works as follows:

(i)   a bonus of 5% of weekly pay for each employee for any week in which the departmental production is more than 10% above the target production for the week

(ii)   a bonus of $1 per employee for every unit of production produced by that employee over 800 per week.

In one week the departmental target was 40,000 units and 45,000 units were produced. Of these Percy produced 780 and Peter 840. Percy has a basic weekly wage of $240 and Peter $260.

What is the gross pay for each employee that week?

	Percy	Peter
(A)	$252	$313
B	$252	$326
C	$264	$313
D	$264	$326

Handwritten working:
Percy = 240
5% = 12
= 252

Peter = 260
5% = 13
Production bonus = 40
= 313

198 Anish manufactures wooden pallets and employs people on a piece rate scheme of $2.00 per pallet made. If an employee produces more than 200 pallets in a week, any extra pallets made over 200 are paid at a rate of $3.00 per pallet. All employees have a guaranteed minimum weekly wage of $375.

Last week an employee produced 235 pallets.

What was the employee's gross pay for last week?

A $400

B $375

C $505

D $370

$200 \times 2.0 = 400$

$35 \times 3.0 = 105$

$= 505$

199 **How is income tax deducted from employees' salaries accounted for?**

A   An asset and a liability

B   A liability and an expense

C   Income and an asset

D   An expense and an asset

200 **How often will a business usually remit income tax to the taxation authority?**

A   Weekly

B   Monthly

C   Quarterly

D   Annually

201 **What does the labour cost charged in the profit and loss account of a business consist of?**

A   Gross pay

B   Gross pay plus employer's state benefit contributions

C   Gross pay less income tax, employee's state benefit contributions and employer's state benefit contributions

D   Gross pay less income tax and employee's state benefit contributions, plus employer's state benefit contributions

202 Sophie's annual salary is $15,000. She is paid four-weekly and is allowed eight weeks annual leave.

What will be the gross pay on each of her payslips?

A $1,500.00

B $1,363.64

C $1,250.00

D $1,153.85

$4/52 \times 15000$

203 Trevor's basic working week is 40 hours, and his basic rate of pay is $7 per hour. Overtime is paid at the rate of time and a half. In a given week, Trevor worked 46 hours.

What was Trevor's gross pay be for that week?

A $301

B $343

C $385

D $483

40 × 7 = 280
6 × 10·5 = 63
= 343

204 Danny is a salesman, selling medical equipment. He receives a commission of 2% of all sales plus 0.5% of sales of individual items over $20,000 each, and a further 1% on sales exceeding $70,000 a month.

During July, Danny's sales totalled $90,000, including two large machines with selling prices of $18,000 and $22,000 each.

What commission was paid to Danny for July?

A $4,700

B $4,000

C $2,810

D $2,110

Danny = 2% of 90,000
Expensive items = 0·5% of 22,000
Sales over 70,000 = 90,000 - 70,000 × 1%

205 Tommy's basic working week is 38 hours, and his basic rate of pay is $7.50 per hour. Overtime hours are paid at 125% of the normal hourly rate.

Last week Tommy worked 44 hours. What was his gross pay for that week?

A $273.00

B $345.00

C $341.25

D $431.25

Basic = 38 × 7·50 = 285
6 × 9 37 = 56.25

206 **Which of the following is NOT a payroll function?**

A   Calculation of gross pay

B   Notification of holiday entitlement

C   Calculation of tax and other deductions

D   Distributing pay slips

207 **By which of the following would it be unlikely to analyse the payroll?**

A   Geographical area

B   Department

C   Home address

D   Factory

208 Which of the following is NOT used to authorise pay?

A   Countersigned time sheets

B   Job cards confirmed by managers

Ⓒ   Self-certified work sheets

D   Weekly time sheets signed by management

209 An employee believes that he has been underpaid. How can payroll staff check this?

A   By asking the tax authorities (The taxation authorities)

B   By looking at the payslip provided

C   By asking the employee's manager

Ⓓ   By looking through the payroll documentation

210 Which of the following accounts is NOT used in the payroll function?

A   Bank

Ⓑ   Drawings

C   Pension payable

D   Wages and salaries expense

CONTROL ACCOUNTS, BANK RECONCILIATIONS AND THE INITIAL TRIAL BALANCE

211 Who should NOT prepare a payables control account?

A   Accounts supervisor

Ⓑ   Purchases day book clerk

C   Sales day book clerk

D   Assistant accountant

212 Which of the following is NOT a purpose of control accounts?

The control account is a check, not a replacement for individual ledger accounts

A   Provide a total of receivables and payables at any time

Ⓑ   Avoid preparation of receivables' ledger accounts

C   Identify errors in the day books and postings to the general ledger

D   Check the accuracy of entries in the individual accounts

213 Which of the following is NOT a statement which reconciles or controls?

A   Bank reconciliation statement

B   Control account

Ⓒ   Computerised ledger account

D   Trial balance

214 What is the signature of the buying department manager to authorise a purchase invoice prior to the preparation of a cheque for payment, an example of?

(A) Control

B Recording

C Reconciliation

D Coding

215 After checking a business cash book against the bank statement, which of the following items could require an entry in the cash book?

1 Bank charges

2 A cheque from a customer which was dishonoured

3 Cheque not presented

4 Deposits not credited

5 Credit transfer entered in bank statement

6 Standing order entered in bank statement

(A) Items 1, 2, 5 and 6 only

B Items 3 and 4 only

C Items 1, 3, 4 and 6 only

D Items 3, 4, 5 and 6 only

216 Phillip's bank reconciliation statement shows outstanding lodgements paid in by Phillip of $3,800 and outstanding cheques to suppliers of $3,500. His bank account in his ledger shows a debit balance of $25,000.

What balance does Phillip's bank statement show?

A $25,000

(B) $24,700

C $25,300

D $32,300

25,000 + 3500 − 3800

217 The balance on the cash account for a business at the end of June was an overdraft of $89.93. At that date there were also unpresented cheques totalling $154.38 and an outstanding deposit of $60.00. It was also discovered that during the month of June the bank had charged the business interest on its overdraft for the previous quarter of $16.45.

What is the correct balance on the cash account at the end of June?

A $73.48 overdrawn

(B) $106.38 overdrawn

C $167.86 overdrawn

D $200.76 overdrawn

−89.93 − 16.45

218 The following attempt at a bank reconciliation statement has been prepared by Reg:

	$
Overdraft per bank statement	38,600
Add: deposits not credited	41,200
	79,800
Less: outstanding cheques	3,300
Overdraft per cash book	$76,500

Handwritten: −38600−41,200 = 2600

Handwritten: 3300 − 2600 = 700

Assuming the bank statement balance of $38,600 is correct, what should the cash book balance be?

A $76,500 overdrawn

B $5,900 overdrawn

(C) $700 overdrawn

D $5,900 cash at bank

219 **Which of the following items would you adjust the cash book for when preparing a bank reconciliation statement?**

(i) Outstanding deposits

(ii) Unpresented cheques

(iii) Standing order payment omitted

(iv) Bank charges

A (i) and (ii)

B (i) and (iv)

C (i), (ii) and (iv)

(D) (iii) and (iv)

220 The bank statement shows a balance at the bank of $1,360, whilst the cash book balance on the same date is $1,250.

How could this discrepancy be explained?

A Uncredited lodgement of $110

B Bank charges of $110 not yet recorded in the cash book

(C) Bank interest received of $55 credited in the cash book

D A dishonoured cheque for $55 which the business did not know about until it was returned, after the date of the bank statement

221 A business has a debit balance on its cash book of $148.00 but the bank statement shows a different balance. The following items have also been discovered:

(i) the bank statement shows that there were bank charges for the period of $10 which have not been recorded in the cash account

(ii) a standing order payment for $25 has also been mistakenly omitted from the cash account

(iii) cheques totalling $125 had been written and sent to suppliers but had not yet been presented

(iv) a cheque for $85 had been paid into the bank but was still outstanding.

What is the balance on the bank statement?

A $73

B $113

C $153

D $223

148 - 10 - 25 + 125 - 85

222 The bank statement shows an overdraft of $210. Uncredited lodgements are $30 and unpresented cheques are $83. A dishonoured cheque for $28 was included on the bank statement but has not yet been written into the cash book.

What is the correct cash book balance?

A $263 overdrawn

B $235 overdrawn

C $157 overdrawn

D $129 overdrawn

Balance per bank statement (210)
Less: unpresented cheques (83)
Add: uncredited lodgements 30
corrected balance per cashbook (263)

223 On 31 December Jolyon's cash book shows a balance of $293. The bank statement for 31 December shows a balance of $151.

What could this difference be due to?

A Uncredited lodgements for which adjustment to the cash book is necessary

B Uncredited lodgements for which no adjustment to the cash book is necessary

C Bank interest received as revealed by the bank statement, for which adjustment to the cash book is necessary

D Bank interest received as revealed by the bank statement, for which no adjustment to the cash book is necessary

224 At 1 March, the cash book showed a balance of $850. Transactions during March were:

	$
Cash sales	230
Credit sales	1,950
Cheques written	1,200
Remittance from receivables	1,500

What was the cash book balance at 31 March?

A $1,380

B $1,830

C $3,100

D $3,330

225 At 1 April the bank statement showed a balance of $950. Reconciling items on the bank reconciliation statement were unpresented cheques of $100 and a bank error comprising bank charges overcharged to the extent of $20. During April, cheques and deposits appearing on the bank statement were $1,600 and $1,900 respectively. At 30 April the only reconciling items were unpresented cheques of $210.

What was the cash book balance at 30 April?

A $960

B $1,040

C $1,060

D $1,120

226 Which of the following statements is true in relation to uncredited lodgements?

A They constitute an error in the cash book

B They constitute an error in the bank statement

C They result from the cash book being out of date compared with the bank statement

D They result from the bank statement being out of date compared with the cash book

227 How often should a bank reconciliation statement be prepared for a large retail group?

A Annually

B Monthly

C Daily

D Weekly

228 Which of the following items would not affect a bank reconciliation?

A Dishonoured cheque

B Discount received

C Bank interest

D Lodgements not presented

229 A cheque appears in the bank statement the same day as it appears in the cash book. Why would this occur?

   A   It has been posted to the payee

   (B) It has been used to withdraw cash for wages

   C   It has passed through the bank clearing system

   D   It represents payment to a shopkeeper in a foreign country

230 Which document in a well-run sole trader business should show the same balance as recorded in the business cash book?

   (A) The latest cheque book counterfoil

   B   The bank statement

   C   The paying in book

   D   The petty cash book

231 Which transaction is recorded in the bank before the business cash book?

   A   A cashed cheque

   B   Payment of a credit card bill

   (C) Bank charges

   D   A cash sale

232 Which of the following would not appear in a bank statement?

   (A) A credit card purchase

   B   A debit card purchase

   C   A BACS transfer to pay wages

   D   An EFTPOS transfer for an internet sale

233 The trade receivables' control account balance is $1,000 and the total of the individual trade receivables' balances is $850.

   Which of the following errors could account for this difference?

   A   A receipt from a credit customer $150 was recorded twice in the receivables' ledger and control account

   B   A receipt from a credit customer $150 was not recorded at all in the receivables' ledger

   (C) A receipt from a credit customer $150 was not recorded at all in the control account

   D   A receipt from a credit customer $150 was recorded twice in the control account

234 Which of the following items would NOT lead to a difference between the total of the balances on the accounts receivable ledger and the balance on the receivables' ledger control account?

    A   An error in totalling the sales day book

    B   An error in totalling the receipts column of the cash book

    C   An overstatement of an entry in an accounts receivable account

    (D)   An entry posted to the wrong account receivable account

235 The receivables' ledger control account at 1 May had a balance of $32,750. During May, sales of $125,000 were made on credit. Receipts from receivables amounted to $122,500 and there were contras with the payables' ledger control account of $550 were allowed. Refunds of $1,300 were made to customers.

What is the closing balance at 31 May on the receivables' ledger control account?

    (A) $33,400 debit

    B $34,500 debit

    C $36,000 debit

    D $37,100 debit

236 The balance on a business's receivables' ledger control account was $1,586. It was then discovered that the sales day book for the period had been undercast by $100 and the cash book receipts had been overcast by $100.

What is the correct balance on the receivables' ledger control account?

    A $1,386

    B $1,586

    C $1,686

    (D) $1,786

237 Vic's receivables' ledger balances add up to $50,000, which does not agree with his receivables' control account.

What should the total of the balances on his receivables' ledger be after correcting the following errors?

    1   A bank credit transfer from a credit customer of $750 was not recorded in the receivables' ledger.

    2   A contra entry of $2,000 was entered in the control account but not in the receivables' and payables' ledgers.

    A $52,750

    B $50,000

    C $49,250

    (D) $47,250

238 Receivables at 1 April were $8,450. Transactions during the month were credit sales of $19,600, cheques received from receivables of $22,430, sales returns of $1,000 and a contra with a credit supplier of $540.

What was the balance on the receivables' control account at 30 April?

A $4,080

B $4,620

C $6,080

D $12,820

Handwritten annotation:

RCA

1 April 8450	Cheques 22430
Sales 19600	Returns 1000
	contra 540

239 Lancelot's receivables, which were $500 on 1 July, rose to $700 at the end of July. During the month he issued cash sales receipts of $280, credit sales invoices of $1,900 and credit notes of $170.

How much cash was received from accounts receivable during July?

A $1,250

B $1,530

C $1,810

D $1,870

Handwritten annotation:

1 July 500	Credit notes 170
Sales invoice 1900	Cash (bal fig) 1530
2400	Balance c/d 700

240 The following information is available about a business:

Opening receivables	$54,550
Closing receivables	$52,560
Receipts from customers in the period	$98,460

Irrecoverable receivables written off during the period $2,000

Of the receipts $16,838 represented cash sales. What is the amount of sales on credit for the period?

A $85,612

B $79,632

C $96,470

D $81,632

Handwritten annotation:

Trade Receivables

Opening bal 54550	Cash received re credit sales 81622
Credit Sales 81632	Irrecoverable w/off 2000
	Balance c/d 52,560
136,182	136,182

241 The following are the year end balances in a business' ledgers:

	$
Sales	628,000
Cost of sales	458,000
General overheads	138,000
Payables	54,000
Receivables	111000 ?
Cash on deposit	61,000
Capital	86,000

Handwritten annotations:
Assets + expenses   Income Liabilities Capital

458,000   628,000
138,000   54,000
61,000   86,000
111,000

If the trial balance balances, what is the missing figure for receivables?

A $61,000

(B) $111,000

C $233,000

D $387,000

242 A debit balance of $250 due from K Ltd was treated as a credit balance in the payables ledger clerk's listing.

Which of the following adjustments would correct this error?

A Reduce the total for all balances by $250

B Increase the total for all balances by $250

(C) Reduce the total for all balances by $500

D Increase the total for all balances by $500

C Make adjustments to the control accounts, with no effect on profit

243 The balance on the payables' ledger control account was $3,446. It was then discovered that the total from the cash book payments during the period had been posted as $14,576 instead of $14,756. It was also discovered that a contra with the receivables' ledger control account of $392 had not been posted at all.

What is the correct balance on the payables' ledger control account?

(A) $2,874

B $3,234

C $3,658

D $4,018

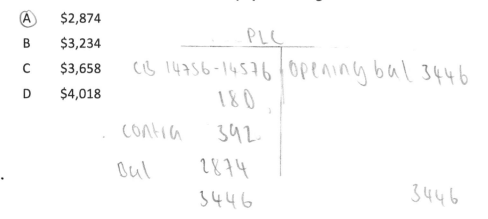

Handwritten working:
PLC
CB 14756-14576   Opening bal 3446
180
contra 392
Bal 2874
3446   3446

244 The following information is available about a business:

Opening payables	$23,450
Closing payables	$25,600
Payments for purchases in the period	$87,350

Of the payments $17,850 represented cash purchases. What is the value of purchases made on credit for the period?

A $85,200

B $67,350

C $89,500

(D) $71,650

245 ANO issued a supplier statement to BNO showing a balance outstanding of $14,350. BNO's records show a balance outstanding of $14,500.

From BNO's perspective, which of the following statements could be a reason that explains this difference?

A   The supplier sent an invoice for $150 which you have not yet received

(B)   The supplier has allowed you $150 cash discount which you had omitted to enter in your ledgers

C   You have paid the supplier $150 which he has not yet accounted for

D   You have returned goods worth $150 which the supplier has not yet accounted for

246 A business had a trade payables' ledger control account balance of $32,750 at 1 May 20X7. During May 20X7, purchases of $125,000 were made on credit, payments made to suppliers amounted to $122,500 and contras with the trade receivables' ledger control account amounted to $1,100. During May 20X7, goods which had cost $1,300 were returned to suppliers, for which credit notes were issued.

What was the balance on the trade payables' ledger control account at 31 May 20X7?

A $35,250

B $35,450

(C) $32,850

D $35,050

247 A business had a trade payables' ledger control account balance at 1 December 20X5 of $52,750. During the year ended 30 November 20X6, purchases of $325,000 were made on credit, payments made to suppliers amounted to $322,500 and early settlement discounts received totalled $5,250. During the year ended 30 November 20X6, goods returned to suppliers totalled $6,500, for which credit notes were issued.

What was the balance on the trade payables' ledger control account at 30 November 20X6?

A $54,000

(B) $43,500

C $56,500

D $67,000

248 A business had a trade payables' ledger control account balance of $34,560 as at 1 July 20X3. During the year ended 30 June 20X4, payments were made to suppliers of $260,000 and purchases made during the same period amounted to $270,000. During the year ended 30 June 20X4, early settlement discounts received totalled $7,500, and faulty goods returned to suppliers totalled $4,500, for which credit notes were issued.

What was the balance on the trade payables' ledger control account at 30 June 20X4?

A $27,560

B $47,560

C $41,560

D $32,560

Handwritten working:

Trade Payables

Cash paid 260,000	1 July 34560
Discounts 7,500	Purchases 270,000
Credit Note 4,500	
Closing bal 32,560	304,560

249 A business had a trade payables' ledger control account balance of $55,555 as at 1 April 20X4. During the year ended 31 March 20X5, purchases made during the year ended 31 March 20X5 amounted to $395,000. During the year ended 31 March 20X5, early settlement discounts received totalled $6,500, faulty goods returned to suppliers totalled $3,500, for which credit notes were issued and early settlement discounts of $6,500 were received. At 31 March 20X5, the total on the trade payables ledger control account was $50,555.

What was the total of payments made to suppliers during the year ended 31 March 20X5?

A $390,000

B $397,000

C $403,000

D $410,000

Handwritten working:

Trade payables ledger control a/c

Discounts 6500	1 April 55,555
Returns 3500	Purchases 395,000
Cash paid 390,000	
Closing bal 50,555	450,555

250 At 31 A business had a trade payables' ledger control account balance of $33,250 as at 1 October 20X2. During the year ended 30 September 20X3, cash paid to settle amounts outstanding for purchases was $335,500. In addition, early settlement discounts received totalled $3,350, faulty goods returned to suppliers totalled $2,500, for which credit notes were issued. At 30 September 20X3, the total on the trade payables' ledger control account was $31,750. March 20X5, the total on the trade payables' ledger control account was $50,555.

What was the total of purchases made on credit during the year ended 30 September 20X3?

A $339,850

B $333,150

C $334,850

D $328,150

Handwritten working:

Trade payables ledger

Discounts 3,350	1 Oct 33,250
Returns 2,500	Purchases 339,850
Cash paid 335,500	
Closing bal 31,750	
373,100	373,100

251 Which of the following errors would be found by extracting a trial balance?

    A   A transaction has been completely missed in the accounts

    B   The double entries have been made the wrong way round

    Ⓒ   Different figures have been entered for the debit and credit entries

    D   An expense item has been posted to a non-current asset account

252 For the month of November 20X0 Figgins Co made purchases at a cost of $225,600 plus sales tax of $33,840. The total of $259,440 has been credited to the payables' ledger control account as $254,940.

Which of the following adjustments will correct the error?

	Control account	List of payables' balances
Ⓐ	$4,500 Cr	No adjustment
B	$4,500 Cr	Increase by $4,500
C	$29,340 Dr	No effect
D	$33,840 Dr	Increase by $4,500

253 Arlene has posted an invoice for equipment repairs of $240 to the building repairs account.

What journal entry and explanation are required to correct this?

    A   Dr   Equipment repairs $240, and   Cr   Building repairs $240

           Being correction of an error of omission – invoice posted to wrong account.

    B   Dr   Building repairs $240, and   Cr   Equipment repairs $240

           Being correction of an error of omission – invoice posted to wrong account

    C   Dr   Building repairs $240, and   Cr   Equipment repairs $240

           Being correction of an error of commission – invoice posted to wrong account

    Ⓓ   Dr   Equipment repairs $240, and   Cr   Building repairs $240

           Being correction of an error of commission – invoice posted to wrong account.

254 Dawn has posted an invoice for $630 to the correct side of the stationery account. The invoice was for advertising.

What journal entry and explanation should be made to correct this?

    A   Dr   Advertising $630, and   Cr   Stationery $630

           Being correction of an error of omission – invoice posted to wrong account

    Ⓑ   Dr   Advertising $630 and   Cr   Stationery $630

           Being correction of an error of commission – invoice posted to wrong account

    C   Dr   Stationery $630, and   Cr   Advertising $630

           Being correction of an error of omission – invoice posted to wrong account

    D   Dr   Stationery $630, and   Cr   Advertising $630

           Being correction of an error of commission – invoice posted to wrong account

255 **Which of the following will NOT cause an entry to be made in a suspense account?**

A   Drawings shown on the credit side of the trial balance

(B)   Discounts received shown on the credit side of the trial balance

C   Omission of an irrecoverable debt written off from the trial balance

D   The entry of cash in hand ($1,680) on the trial balance as $1,860

256 The trial balance of Co did not agree, and a suspense account was opened for the difference. Checking in the bookkeeping system revealed a number of errors:

Error

1      $4,600 paid for motor van repairs was correctly treated in the cash book but was credited to motor vehicles asset account.

2      $360 received from Brown, a customer, was credited in error to the account of Green.

3      $9,500 paid for rent was debited to the rent account as $5,900.

4   An irrecoverable debt of $250 had been debited in error to the purchases account.

5   No entries had been made to record a cash sale of $100.

Which of the errors above would require an entry to the suspense account as part of the process of correcting them?

A   Errors 3 and 4 only

(B)   Errors 1 and 3 only

C   Errors 2 and 5 only

D   Errors 2 and 3 only

257 The following are the year-end balances in Sam's ledgers:

	$	
Sales	43,000 Cr	Debits and credits Balance
Purchases	16,000 Dr	
Equipment	22,000 Dr	
Overdraft	8,000 Cr	
Inventory	19,000 Dr	
Capital	6,000 Cr	

What is the trial balance total?

A $43,000

(B) $57,000

C $63,000

D $114,000

credit = 43,000 + 8000 + 6000 = 57000

Debit = 22,000 + 16000 + 19000 = 57,000

258 A trial balance has been extracted and a suspense account opened. One error related to the mis-posting of an amount of $200, being discounts received from credit suppliers, to the wrong side of the discounts received account.

What will be the correcting journal entry?

A   Dr Discounts received account $200, Cr Suspense account $200

B   Dr Suspense account $200, Cr Discounts received account $200

C   Dr Discounts received account $400, Cr Suspense account $400

D   Dr Suspense account $400, Cr Discounts received account $400

259 The trial balance totals of Gamma at 30 September 20X3 were:

Debit $992,640

Credit $1,026,480

Which TWO of the following possible errors could, when corrected, result with the trial balance to agree?

Error

1   A payment of rent of $6,160 has not been entered in the rent payable account or the cash book.

2   The balance on the motor expenses account $27,680 has incorrectly been listed in the trial balance as a credit.

3    $6,160 proceeds from the sale of a motor vehicle have been posted to the debit of the cash book and the credit of motor vehicles asset account.

4   The balance of $21,520 on the rent receivable account has been omitted from the trial balance.

A   Errors 1 and 2   1,026,480 - 992,640 = 33840

B   Errors 2 and 3

C   Errors 2 and 4

D   Errors 3 and 4

260 The trial balance of Smith did not agree, and a suspense account was opened for the difference. Smith maintains ledger control accounts for receivables' and payables' as part of the double-entry accounting system. The following errors were subsequently identified:

Error

1   A cash refund due to customer A was correctly treated in the cash book and then credited to the receivables' ledger account of customer B.

2   The withdrawal of goods by Smith for own use of $300 was recorded by debiting sales revenue account and crediting purchases.

3   The total of contra between the payables' and receivables' ledger control accounts had been credited in error to the sales account. −

4   Some of the cash received from customers had been used to pay sundry expenses before banking the remaining receipts.

5    $5,800 paid for plant repairs was correctly treated in the cash book and credited to plant and equipment asset account. −

Which of the above errors would require an entry to the suspense account as part of the process of correcting them?

A   Errors 1, 3 and 5 only

B   Errors 1, 2 and 5 only

C   Errors 1 and 5 only

D   Errors 3 and 4 only

261 A suspense account was opened when a trial balance failed to agree. The following errors were later discovered:

Error

1   A gas bill of $420 had been recorded in the Gas account as $240.

2   A contra for $50 between the Receivables' ledger control account and Payables' ledger control accounts had been correctly accounted for in Receivables' ledger control account and credited to the Payables' ledger control account.

3   Interest received of $70 had been entered in the bank account only.

When the errors were correct, the suspense account balance was cleared. What was the original balance on the suspense account?

A   Debit $210

B   Credit $210

C   Debit $160

D   Credit $160

262 On extracting a trial balance, a suspense account is opened with a credit balance on it. You discover that this is caused by a single error in the general (nominal) ledger.

Which of the following could therefore have caused the imbalance?

A   The income tax and social security deductions for the current month have been entered twice in the deductions control account

B   An accounts receivable ledger/accounts payable ledger contra has been entered on the credit side of both control accounts

C   The opening accrual for telephone charges has been brought forward at the beginning of the year on the wrong side of the ledger account

D   The figure of closing inventory has been entered on both sides of the trial balance

263 Jones, a sole trader, has extracted a trial balance and needed to include a suspense account to make it balance. He has discovered the following errors:

Error

1   Opening inventory of $1,475 has been listed in the trial balance as a credit balance of $1,745.

2   The sales for November ($5,390 inclusive of sales tax) had been correctly entered in the control account and the sales account but no entry had been made in the sales tax account. The amount entered in the sales revenue account was $4,600.

3   The opening accrual for telephone charges of $190 had been brought forward on the wrong side of the telephone expense account.

What was the suspense account balance that Jones included in the trial balance?

A $2,050 Dr

B $2,050 Cr

C $2,840 Dr

D $2,840 Cr

(handwritten annotation):
Suspense account
Balance 2050 | inventory (1745+1475) 3220
Telephone 380 |
sales tax 790 |

264 An accountant is attempting to resolve a suspense account difference. One of the errors related to a mis-posting of $3,079 of sales tax on purchases to the wrong side of the sales tax account.

What will be the correcting entry?

A   Debit Sales tax account $6,158, Credit Suspense account $6,158

B   Debit Suspense account $6,158, Credit Sales tax account $6,158

C   Debit Sales tax account $3,079, Credit Suspense account $3,079

D   Debit Suspense account $3,079, Credit Sales tax account $3,079

265 A suspense account shows a credit balance of $130.

What could this be due to?

A   Omitting a sale of $130 from the receivables ledger

(B)   Recording a purchase of $130 twice in the purchases account

C   Failing to write off an irrecoverable debt of $130

D   Recording an electricity bill paid of $65 by debiting the bank account and crediting the electricity account

266 Kim's bookkeeper has posted an invoice for motor repairs to the motor vehicles at cost account.

What term is used to describe this type of error?

A   Error of omission

B   Error of commission

(C)   Error of principle

D   Error of transposition

267 Arlene received a cheque for $450 from her insurance company in settlement of a claim for the cost of repairs to a van. The bookkeeper recorded the cheque correctly in the cash book, but did not complete the double entry. The totals of the trial balance did not agree and a suspense account was opened to record the difference.

What journal entry is required to eliminate the balance on the suspense account?

(A)   Dr   Suspense $450, and   Cr   Insurance $450

     Being correction of an error of omission

B   Dr   Insurance $450, and   Cr   Suspense $450

     Being correction of an error of omission

C   Dr   Suspense $450, and   Cr   Van repairs $450

     Being correction of an error of omission

D   Dr   Van Repairs $450, and   Cr   Suspense $450

     Being correction of an error of omission

268 Which of the following items would normally be a credit balance in the trial balance?

(i) Bank loan

(ii) Owner's capital

(iii) Drawings

(iv) Purchases

A (i) and (ii)

B (i) and (iii)

C (ii) and (iii)

D (ii) and (iv)

269 Which of the following balances would appear on the same side in the trial balance?

A Drawings and trade payables

B Drawings and purchases

C Owner's capital and purchases

D Owner's capital and rent

270 Which of the following pairs of balances would appear on the same side of a trial balance?

(i) bank loan and cash in hand

(ii) Trade receivables and purchases

(iii) Trade payables and purchases

(iv) Bank loan and trade payables

A (i) and (ii)

B (ii) and (iii)

C (ii) and (iv)

D (iii) and (iv)

271 Which of the following statements describes a compensating error?

A They are not revealed by the preparation of a trial balance and do not necessitate adjustment.

B They are not revealed by the preparation of a trial balance and do necessitate adjustment.

C They are revealed by the preparation of a trial balance and do not necessitate adjustment.

D They are revealed by the preparation of a trial balance and do necessitate adjustment.

272 During January, the accounts clerk made two mistakes when recording the accounting entries. Firstly, motor expenses of $50 were debited to the motor vehicles account. Secondly, $200 cash received from an account receivable was debited to an account payable account. The other halves of both of these double entries were posted correctly.

When the trial balance was extracted at 31 January, by how much did the debit side of the trial balance exceed the credit side?

A $450

B $400

C $250

D $200

273 An invoice to a customer, M Smith, has been recorded in the receivable account of N Smith.

What type of error is this?

A Error of commission

B Error of principle

C Error of omission

D An error of original entry

274 **When would a trial balance NOT agree?**

A When the bank reconciliation indicates there are outstanding items in the clearing system.

B When the receivables' ledger control account indicates there is a contra item with the payables ledger control account.

C When a supplier statement omits an invoice for goods received.

D When the analysis columns in the petty cash book have not been recorded in the general ledger.

275 A bookkeeper made the following errors when recording transactions:

1 A cash payment of $100 for stationery had not entered in the books at all.

2 A discount received of $30 was entered in the debit side of discounts received account and correctly posted to the trade payables ledger control account.

3 $300 cash drawings were debited in the repairs expense account and correctly posted in the cash book.

What is the balance on the suspense account before these errors are corrected?

A $30 credit

B $100 debit

C $300 credit

D $60 credit

276 **Which of the following accounting entries is incorrect?**

    A   Dr Cash; Cr Sales revenue

    B   Dr Motor vehicle; Cr Capital

    C   Dr Purchases; Cr Account payable (payable)

    (D)   Dr Trial balance; Cr Bank

Trial balance is a list of balances not part of a double entry system

277 The purchases day book of Arbroath has been undercast by $500, and the sales day book has been overcast by $700. Arbroath maintains payables' and receivables' ledger control accounts as part of the double entry bookkeeping system.

    How will these errors be corrected?

    A   Make adjustments to the ledger balances of the individual receivables' and payables', with no effect on profit

    B   Make adjustments to the ledger balances of the individual receivables' and payables', with a decrease in profit of $1,200

    C   Make adjustments to the control accounts, with no effect on profit

    (D)   Make adjustments to the control accounts, with a decrease in profit of $1,200.

278 **The transfer journal would be most likely to be used as the book of prime entry to record which of the following double entries?**

    A   A cash sale

    B   The payment of a supplier

    (C)   The purchase of a non-current asset

    D   Discount received

279 The rental payment for the quarter has been recorded in the ledger accounts as an insurance expense.

    What type of error is this?

    (A)   Error of commission

    B   Error of principle

    C   Error of omission

    D   An error of original entry

280 **What does a trial balance indicate?**

    A   That all the transactions have been entered

    B   That every entry is correct

    (C)   That an equal value of debits and credits has been posted into the accounting ledgers

    D   That all necessary accounts have been opened

Section 3

ANSWERS TO STUDY SUPPORT QUESTIONS

BUSINESS TRANSACTIONS AND DOCUMENTATION

1   CASH OR CREDIT

TRANSACTION		CASH	CREDIT
(a)	Receipt of goods worth $140.59 from a supplier together with an invoice for that amount.		✓
(b)	Payment of $278.50 by cheque for a purchase at the till.	✓	
(c)	Receipt of a deposit of $15.00 for goods.	✓	
(d)	Sending of an invoice for $135.00 to the payer of the deposit for the remaining value of the goods.		✓
(e)	Sale of goods for $14.83, payment received by credit card.	✓	

2   DOCUMENTS

(a)   Order

(b)   Purchase invoice

(c)   Remittance advice

(d)   Credit note

(e)   Cash receipt

3   DEBIT/CREDIT NOTES

A credit note is a document produced by the **supplier** and sent to the **customer** which cancels all or part of **an invoice**.

A debit note, on the other hand, is raised by the **customer** and sent to the **supplier** requesting a **credit note**. Not all businesses employ a formal debit note for this purpose; many rely on a letter or telephone call only.

DOUBLE ENTRY BOOKKEEPING

4 TERMINOLOGY

(a) An **asset** is a present resource controlled by the **entity** as a result of a past **event**.

(b) A **liability** is an amount owed by the business to another business or individual.

Examples include a **loan from a bank** and amounts owed to the suppliers of goods or services which have yet to be paid for – payables.

(c) **Inventory** is an asset comprising goods purchased for resale, components for inclusion in manufactured products, and the finished products which have been manufactured which have not yet been sold.

(d) **Capital** is the liability of the business to the owner of the business.

(e) **Drawings** is the term which refers to amounts taken out of the business by the owner.

5 CLASSIFYING TRANSACTIONS AND BALANCES

(a) Asset – inventory

(b) Expense

(c) Income

(d) Asset – trade receivables

(e) Expense

(f) Liability (this is a special liability known as capital)

(g) Liability – payables

(h) Asset

(i) Asset

(j) Income

(k) Asset

6 BILL SMITH – ACCOUNTING EQUATION

(a) Bill Smith starts a new business by putting $10,000 into a business bank account.

Assets =	Capital	+ Profit	– Drawings	+ Liabilities
10,000	10,000			

(b) A bank lends the business a further $5,000.

Assets =	Capital	+ Profit	– Drawings	+ Liabilities
15,000	10,000			5,000

(c) Bill buys a delivery van for $6,000.

Assets =	Capital	+ Profit	– Drawings	+ Liabilities
15,000	10,000			5,000

Although the accounting equation looks the same as in (b) above, the assets now consist of cash at bank ($9,000) and van ($6,000).

(d)   Bill buys inventory for $2,500 by writing out a business cheque.

Assets =	Capital	+ Profit	− Drawings	+ Liabilities
15,000	10,000			5,000

Although the accounting equation looks the same as in (b) above, the assets now consist of cash at bank ($6,500), inventory ($2,500) and van ($6,000).

(e)   All the inventory is sold for $4,000. The money is paid direct to the business bank account.

Step 1 Work out profit

	$
Sales	4,000
Cost of sales	2,500
	———
Profit	1,500
	———

Step 2 Insert into accounting equation

Assets =	Capital	+ Profit	− Drawings	+ Liabilities
16,500	10,000	1,500		5,000

The assets now consist of cash at bank ($10,500) and van ($6,000).

Conclusion

Remember that all of the $4,000 sales proceeds is paid into the bank account.

(f)   Bill pays a business expense of $400 out of the business bank account.

Step 1 Work out new profit

	$
Sales	4,000
Expenses	
Cost of sales	(2,500)
Sundry expenses	(400)
	———
Profit	1,100
	———

Step 2 Insert into accounting equation

Assets =	Capital	+ Profit	− Drawings	+ Liabilities
16,100	10,000	1,100		5,000

The assets now consist of cash at bank ($10,100) and van ($6,000).

(g)   Finally Bill takes $300 out of the business for his own purposes.

Assets =	Capital	+ Profit	− Drawings	+ Liabilities
15,800	10,000	1,100	(300)	5,000

Cash at bank is now reduced to $9,800. The other remaining asset is the van ($6,000).

7   BANNER'S BOOKS – LEDGER ACCOUNTS

Transactions	Account to be debited	Account to be credited
(a)	Bank	Capital
(b)	Purchases	Bank
(c)	Bank (or cash)	Sales
(d)	Rent	Bank
(e)	Van	Bank

8   CAMERON FINDLAY – LEDGER ACCOUNTS

Cash at bank account

		$			$
(a)	Capital a/c	1,500	(b)	Rent a/c	230
(e)	Sales a/c	240	(c)	Purchases a/c	420
(g)	Sales a/c	16	(d)	Purchases a/c	180
(j)	Sales a/c	50	(f)	Purchases a/c	10
			(h)	Purchases a/c	80
			(i)	Wages a/c	95
			(k)	Sundry expenses a/c	10
				Balance c/d	781
		_____			_____
		1,806			1,806
		_____			_____
	Balance b/d	781			

Capital account

		$			$
			(a)	Cash at bank a/c	1,500

Rent account

		$			$
(b)	Cash at bank a/c	230			

Purchases account

		$			$
(c)	Cash at bank a/c	420			
(d)	Cash at bank a/c	180			
(f)	Cash at bank a/c	10			
(h)	Cash at bank a/c	80		Balance c/d	690
		———			———
		690			690
		———			———
	Balance b/d	690			

Sales account

		$			$
			(e)	Cash at bank a/c	240
			(g)	Cash at bank a/c	16
	Balance c/d	306	(j)	Cash at bank a/c	50
		———			———
		306			306
		———			———
				Balance b/d	306

Wages account

		$		$
(i)	Cash at bank a/c	95		

Sundry expenses account

		$		$
(k)	Cash at bank a/c	10		

Tutorial note

It is not necessary to perform the mechanics of balancing an account which contains only one entry as this entry is the balance.

9 JOHN FRY – LEDGER ACCOUNTS AND BALANCING

Cash and bank account

	$		$
Capital	10,000	Van	3,600
Sales	110	Van	1,700
Sales	80	Purchases	400
Sales	170	Freezer	260
Sales	50	Purchases	190
		Wages	40
		Drawings	60
		Bal c/d	4,160
	10,410		10,410

Capital account

	$		$
Bal c/d	10,000	Cash and bank	10,000
	10,000		10,000

Van account

	$		$
Cash and bank	3,600		
Cash and bank	1,700	Bal c/d	5,300
	5,300		5,300

Purchases account

	$		$
Cash and bank	400		
Cash and bank	190	Bal c/d	590
	590		590

Sales account

	$		$
		Cash and bank	110
		Cash and bank	80
		Cash and bank	170
Bal c/d	**410**	Cash and bank	50
	410		410

Freezer account

	$		$
Cash and bank	260	**Bal c/d**	**260**
	260		260

Wages

	$		$
Cash and bank	40	**Bal c/d**	**40**
	40		40

Drawings

	$		$
Cash and bank	60	**Bal c/d**	**60**
	60		60

10   ASSETS OR LIABILITIES?

(a)   Asset

(b)   Asset

(c)   Liability

(d)   Asset

(e)   Liability

(f)   Asset

(g)   Asset

BANKING AND PETTY CASH

11   PETTY CASH PRACTICE

PETTY CASH BOOK

Date 20X4	Receipts $	Voucher/ reference no.	Details	Total payment $	Sales tax $	Office expenses $	Travel expenses $	Postage $	Stationery $	Sundry $
1 Aug	126.58		Balance b/d							
1 Aug	73.42		Cash from bank							
1 Aug		279	Refreshments	11 78		11 78				
1 Aug		280	Taxi	3 90			3 90			
2 Aug		281	Window cleaners	26 00		26 00				
3 Aug		282	Client lunch	27 90	4 16					23 74
3 Aug		283	Stamps	11 00				11 00		
4 Aug		284	Stationery	19 49	2 90				16 59	
4 Aug		285	Rail fare	12 00			12 00			
4 Aug		286	Stamps	2 30				2 30		
				114 37	7 06	37 78	15 90	13 30	16 59	23 74
7 Aug	200		Balance c/d	85 63						
				200 00						
7 Aug	85.63		Balance b/d							
8 Aug	114.37		Cash from bank							

12   IMPREST SYSTEM

Payments out of petty cash will occur when an authorised **petty cash voucher** and supporting **receipts** are produced. Properly evidenced vouchers are **authorised** by senior members of staff.

At the end of the month the petty cash payments will **equal** the vouchers and their supporting documentation, and a cheque will be cashed at the bank for this amount so as to replenish the **imprest**.

The vouchers etc. will be removed and **filed** after having been recorded in the **petty cash book**. The vouchers, cash and petty cash records are held securely in a box and preferably in a **safe**.

13   BANKING SERVICES

Standing orders and direct debits are both methods of payment whereby the bank is instructed to pay a third party from a bank account. However, the main difference is as follows:

(i)   with a **standing order** it is the payer who instructs his bank to pay a certain amount on a regular basis to the payee

(ii)   with a **direct debit** it is the payee that instructs the bank of the payment and specifies the amount which may alter for each payment.

Credit cards and debit cards are both methods of making payments used by consumers. However the main difference is as follows:

(i)   a **credit card** is a means of purchasing goods without immediate payment. Payment is made on the total balance outstanding on the card sometime after the purchase has been made

(ii)   a **debit card** is a method of making an immediate payment for purchases but without the need to write out a cheque. On payment with a **debit card** the purchaser's bank account is electronically debited immediately with the amount of the purchase.

14   PARTIES TO A CHEQUE

(a)   AM Baker and JS Baker

(b)   National Southern Bank

(c)   L Fuller

15 BANKING MONEY

It is important to keep cash, cheques and vouchers secure. If any are lost or stolen, this reduces the profits of the organisation. Initially the various items tend to be kept in a **till** and any excess amount should be regularly transferred to a **safe** during the day, keeping actual cash in the **till** to a minimum. Money, vouchers and so on should also be taken to the **bank** regularly to reduce the amount held on premises. This could be daily, every two or three days or other intervals depending on the amount received day to day. Banking should be undertaken **irregularly** so that there is not a regular pattern of visiting the bank.

Paying in slips are used to include details of cash and cheques and, usually separately, card vouchers. If the business accepts a number of cheques, it is usual to supply a **remittance list** which can be checked against the actual cheques by the bank to avoid or resolve problems.

If the home branch of the business is in another city, the amounts paid into the bank will need to travel through the **bank clearing system** which takes several days before it reaches the home branch. On receipt, certain items will be 'cleared' such as **cash**. This amount can be used immediately. Cheques paid into the bank are subject to clearance before the amount they represent can be used as cleared funds. This period provides sufficient time for the cheques to be returned if there are any technical problems with the cheque or there are **insufficient funds** in the account.

If the business has a large number of staff, **BACS** should be used to pay wages and salaries into the bank accounts of the staff members. This reduces the amount of cash that needs to be maintained on the premises and avoids the need to write out numerous cheques or credit transfers.

16 MAINSTREAM CO – CHECKING CORRECTNESS OF REMITTANCES

A number of errors have been made on the remittance advice:

(a)   The invoice number **52843** was for **$316.30** rather than the **$361.30** entered onto the remittance advice.

(b)   The revised cheque total should be:

	$
Invoice 52843	316.30
Invoice 53124	227.00
Invoice 53128	450.20
	——
	993.50
	——

17   ROBERT DEMPSTER – CASH BOOK

(a)

Cash at bank account

		$			$
(a)	Capital	10,000	**(d)**	Vans Galore	**2,000**
(e)	Woodside Rugby Club	65	**(d)**	Surgiplast	**150**
			(f)	**Drawings**	130
				Balance c/d	**7,785**
		———			———
		10,065			10,065
		———			———
	Balance b/d	**7,785**			

(b)   The **separate entity** concept is the principle underlying the treatment of the owner's private expenses paid by the business. This concept requires the transactions of a **business** to be recorded separately from those of the **owner** of a business. Consequently, this payment could not be analysed as 'electricity' as it is not the electricity expense of the business. It may be thought of as a withdrawal of cash from the business by the owner.

SALES AND SALES RECORDS

18   SALES TAX

(a)

Sales tax workings	$
Sales	
Net amount	15,790.00
Sales tax $15,790 \times 17.5\%$	2,763.25
	———
Gross amount	18,553.25
	———
Purchases	
Gross amount	12,455.00
Sales tax $12,455 \times 17.5/117.5$	1,855.00
	———
Net amount	10,600.00
	———

Sales account

	$		$
Bal c/d	**15,790.00**	Receivables (net amount)	**15,790.00**
	15,790.00		**15,790.00**

Receivables account

	$		$
		Cash	13,612.00
Sales (gross amount)	**18,553.25**	Bal c/d	**4,941.25**
	18,553.25		**18,553.25**

Purchases account

	$		$
Payables (net amount)	**10,600.00**	Bal c/d	**10,600.00**
	10,600.00		**10,600.00**

Payables account

	$		$
Cash	9,400.00		
Bal c/d	**3,055.00**	Purchases (gross amt)	**12,455.00**
	12,455.00		**12,455.00**

Sales tax account

	$		$
Sales tax on purchases	**1,855.00**		
Bal c/d	**908.25**	Sales tax on sales	**2,763.25**
	2,763.25		**2,763.25**

(b)   The balance on the sales tax account represents the amount of sales tax that is **owing to** the taxation authorities.

19   VICTORIA LTD – POSTING FROM THE SALES DAY BOOK

Nominal ledger

Sales

	$			$
		30 July	Balance b/d	24,379.20
		3 Aug	SDB	986.86

Receivables ledger control

		$			$
30 July	Balance b/d	1,683.08	30 July	RCB	1,025.18
3 Aug	SDB	1,159.50			

Sales tax

	$			$
		30 July	Balance b/d	352.69
		3 Aug	SDB	172.64

Receivables ledger

Stephen Williams & Co   001

		$		$
30 July	Balance b/d	38.20		
2 Aug	SDB 5109	69.00		

Monty Dee   003

		$			$
30 July	Balance b/d	73.50	2 Aug	RCB	73.50
1 Aug	SDB 5106	61.48			

Roberts Partners				007
	$			$
30 July Balance b/d	279.30	3 Aug RCB		111.62
2 Aug SDB 5107	153.20			

Imogen Jones				009
	$			$
30 July Balance b/d	137.23	30 July RCB		73.20

Olivia Consultants				015
	$			$
30 July Balance b/d	42.61			
1 Aug SDB 5105	82.47			

Anna Pargeter				019
	$			$
30 July Balance b/d	198.17	30 July RCB		204.30
2 Aug SDB 5108	221.78			

Peter Rover				026
	$			$
30 July Balance b/d	296.38			
31 July SDB 5104	142.03			

AM McGee				027
	$			$
30 July Balance b/d	335.28	2 Aug RCB		190.54
SDB 5103	159.30			

Phillipa Steven				032
	$			$
30 July Balance b/d	116.78	31 July RCB		116.78

Clive Brown				035
	$			$
30 July Balance b/d	35.10			
3 Aug SDB 5111	62.70			

Owens Ltd				036
	$			$
30 July Balance b/d	512.74	1 Aug RCB		217.84
3 Aug SDB 5110	159.36			

Cameron Associates				045
	$			$
30 July Balance b/d	335.28	31 July RCB		37.40
SDB 5102	48.18			

20 CREDIT LIMITS

(a) **Customers exceeding their credit limits**

Name	Account	Credit limit	Current balance
		$	$
P Jones & Co	3419284A	21,000	22,457.75
Smith & Co	7143428B	1,700	1,845.45

(b) **Customers with credit limits in excess of $20,000**

Name	Account	Credit limit	Current balance
		$	$
ZLT Ltd	1178947A	35,000	17,171.27
P Jones & Co	3419284A	21,000	22,457.75
Cozens & Sons	6143448A	21,000	18,934.21

(c) Action which can be taken to chase outstanding debts can range from **reminder letters** and **telephone calls** to **legal action** and, eventually, taking a decision to **write the amount off as a bad debt**. Such action must be seriously considered and appropriately authorised by management.

21 LANCING LTD – AGED RECEIVABLES ANALYSIS

Aged receivable listing

Customer	< 30 days $	< 60 days $	<90 days $	> 90 days $	Total $
Vinehall Ltd	72.48	–	28.36	53.81	154.65
Cranbrook Ltd	227.71	–	128.27	–	355.98
Skinners Ltd	–	265.39	103.46	55.35	424.20
Bickley Ltd	61.32	39.37	–	–	100.69
	361.51	304.76	260.09	109.16	1,035.52

Tutorial note

Where possible, you should match a payment to an invoice. For example, Cranbrook Ltd's payment on 25 February for $117.25 and so clearly relates to the invoice dated 15 February. Where it is not possible to match a payment to an invoice, for example where a receivable has only made a part payment, the payment should be allocated to the earliest outstanding invoice.

PURCHASES AND PURCHASE RECORDS

22 POSTING CREDIT TRANSACTIONS

Transactions	Account to be debited	Account to be credited
(a)	Bank	Capital
(b)	Purchases	Accounts payable
(c)	Purchases	Bank
(d)	Rent	Bank
(e)	Accounts receivable	Sales revenue
(f)	Bank	Sales revenue
(g)	Wages	Bank
(h)	Bank	Loan
(i)	Furniture	Accounts payable
(j)	Bank	Accounts receivable
(k)	Accounts payable	Bank

23 SETTLEMENT DISCOUNTS

Accounts receivable

	$		$
Sales	873	Cash at bank account	873

Sales account

	$		$
		Accounts receivable	873

Accounts payable

	$		$
Cash at bank account	582	Purchases of inventory	600
Discounts received	18		

Discounts received account

	$		$
		Accounts payable	18

Purchases account

	$		$
Accounts payable	600		

Cash at bank account

	$		$
Accounts receivable	873	Accounts payable	582

24 GEER & CO – POSTING FROM THE PURCHASE DAY BOOK

NOMINAL LEDGER:

Purchases

		$		$
8 May	Balance b/d	1,652.30		
12 May	PDB	388.00		

Payables ledger control

		$				$
			8 May	Balance b/d		912.36
12 May	CPB	477.20	12 May	PDB		455.87

Sales tax

		$				$
12 May	PDB	67.87	8 May	Balance b/d		80.41

PAYABLE LEDGER:

AD Gosling   003

		$				$
			8 May	Balance b/d		21.73
			12 May	PDB 02268		28.70

Rutland Ltd   006

		$				$
12 May	CPB 03365	149.37	8 May	Balance b/d		149.37

Hopkins Ltd   008

		$				$
12 May	CPB 03363	102.64	8 May	Balance b/d		198.37
				PDB G228		128.39

BA Johnson   012

		$				$
			8 May	Balance b/d		—
			9 May	PDB 2294		33.71

PGE Ltd   015

		$				$
12 May	CPB 03366	93.70	8 May	Balance b/d		117.38
			10 May	PDB 29145		105.29

	Flute Brothers				**017**
		$			$
			8 May	Balance b/d	88.29
			9 May	PDB 82456	48.26

	Brass & Co				**021**
		$			$
8 May	CPB 03362	37.90	8 May	Balance b/d	37.90
			10 May	PDB X8/09	51.26

	SC Basson				**023**
		$			$
10 May	CPB 03364	93.59	8 May	Balance b/d	93.59

	Priddle & Sons				**025**
		$			$
			8 May	Balance b/d	–
			12 May	PDB 0135	60.26

25 RETURNING GOODS

Iqbal must check that his recollection is correct by referring to the **original order**. This could be a copy of a **written** order, a note of a **telephone** order or an **email** confirmation of an order over the internet. If he is right, he should **contact the supplier** to ensure that the correct goods are delivered and the unwanted ones taken back. If there is a delay in delivering the correct goods, he should ask the suppliers to provide a **credit note** so that he will not be charged for the unwanted goods.

PAYROLL

26 PAYROLL KNOWLEDGE

(a) True.

(b) False – but only just! Most employees are entitled to a written statement, but in a few cases, e.g. employees working less than one month – this is not necessary. (The legislation may be different in various countries outside the UK.)

(c) False. Certain responsibilities are implicit, even if they are not stated in the written contract. For example, the duty to exercise reasonable care and skill.

(d) False, for example: such records must be maintained for at least three years in the UK.

27 GROSS PAY – SALARIED AND PIECEWORK

(a) Henry's salary increase occurred two thirds of the way through the month. His gross pay for June is calculated as follows:

	$
$\frac{1}{12} \times \$8,500 \times \frac{2}{3}$	472.22
$\frac{1}{12} \times \$9,000 \times \frac{1}{3}$	250.00
	722.22

(b) Eliza's production is 630 units. Her gross pay is:

$\frac{630}{10} \times \$0.85 =$ **$53.55**

(c) Eliza's production is 700 units. Her gross pay is:

		$
Basic pay	$\frac{700}{10} \times \$0.85$	59.50
Bonus (50 units)	$\frac{50}{10} \times \$1.05$	5.25
		64.75

28 GROSS PAY – OVERTIME

(a) Sandra's hourly rate of pay is:

$\$14,820 \times \frac{1}{52} \times \frac{1}{37.5} = \$7.60$

Her overtime rate is $\$7.60 \times 1.5 = \$11.40$

	$
Her gross pay for the week is:	
Basic pay $\$14,820 \times \frac{1}{52}$	285.00
Overtime hours $(9 - 5)$ @ $\$11.40$	45.60
Gross pay	330.60

(b) (i) Overtime pay = $7 \times \$5.20 \times 1.5 =$ $54.60

(ii) Overtime pay:

4 hours @ $(\$5.20 \times 1.25)$	26.00
3 hours @ $(\$5.20 \times 1.5)$	23.40
	49.40

(iii) Overtime rate $= \$10,010 \times \frac{1}{52} \times \frac{1}{35} = \$5.50$

Overtime pay $= 7 \times \$5.50 = \$38.50$

29   PAYSLIP

Your answer might have included:

(a)   the employer's name

(b)   the employee's name and tax information

(c)   the date

(d)   the total gross pay for this pay day and to date

(e)   the total tax paid for this pay day and to date

(f)   the net pay.

30   PAYROLL ACCOUNTS

Your answer should mention the bank or cash account. Other accounts depend on the systems used and the legislation in the country in which the payroll is prepared. Typical accounts in your answer might be:

(a)   wages and salaries expense

(b)   wages and salaries control

(c)   the tax authorities

(d)   pension payable

(e)   various non-statutory deductions.

CONTROL ACCOUNTS, BANK RECONCILIATIONS AND THE INITIAL TRIAL BALANCE

31   PHILPOTT AND SONS – SELECTING TRANSACTIONS FOR BANK RECONCILIATION

(a)   Adjustment to **cash book** required: the standing order has been omitted.

(b)   **Reconciling item**: this is an unpresented cheque at 31 October.

(c)   Adjustment to **cash book** required: the customer's bank have not honoured this cheque. Therefore the cheque has been sent back to Philpott and Sons' bank who have reduced Philpott and Sons' bank balance accordingly. Philpott and Sons did not know about the cheque at 31 October and so will need to amend their records by making a credit entry in the cash book. This credit will thus cancel the original debit made on receipt of the cheque.

(d)   **Reconciling item**: this is a bank error; the bank should be contacted immediately to correct this mistake.

(e)   **Reconciling item**: these lodgements were outstanding at 31 October.

32   PREPARING A BANK RECONCILIATION STATEMENT

(a)   **Bank reconciliation statement at 31 May 20X4**

	$
Balance per bank statement	1,434.41
Less: Unpresented cheques	(394.67)
	1,039.74
Add: Outstanding lodgements	936.03
Balance per cash book (working)	1,975.77

Working:

Cash at bank account

	$		$
Balance b/d	2,369.37	**Direct debit payment**	**393.60**
		Balance c/d	**1,975.77**
	2,369.37		2,369.37
Balance b/d	**1,975.77**		

(b)   The regular preparation of bank reconciliations serves as a **check** on both the organisation's records and those of the bank.

The bank reconciliation may highlight **differences** between the bank statement and the cash book and these can then be **investigated** and the organisation's and bank's records **brought up to date**.

Bank reconciliations also serve as a check on the time taken to bank lodgements and for them to **clear** through the banking system.

Finally cheques that have been drawn but not yet **presented** can also be monitored in this way.

33   ANDREWS LTD – RECONCILING THE RECEIVABLES LEDGER CONTROL ACCOUNT

Receivables ledger control

		$				$
30 Nov	Balance b/d	25,390.27	31 Mar	Error		27.00
				Irrecoverable debt		169.30
				Balance c/d		25,193.97
		25,390.27				25,390.97

Total of receivable balances

	$
Original total	24,993.57
P Hull balance omitted	227.40
Transposition error	(27.00)
Amended total	25,193.97

Tutorial notes

(a)   *As this balance was omitted from the list of individual receivable balances, it must be added into the original total in order to find the correct receivables figure.*

(b)   *Although this error means that both the accounts of M Skinner and H Skinner show incorrect balances this has no effect on the total of the individual balances.*

(c)   *The invoice that was incorrectly entered into the sales day book affects both the total amount posted to the receivables ledger control account and the individual invoice posted to the individual receivable account.*

(d)   *The irrecoverable debt must be written off in the receivables ledger control account as well as the individual account.*

34   A CLIENT – PREPARING A PAYABLES CONTROL ACCOUNT

(a)

Payables control account

		$			$
(iii)	Credit note	372	(i)	Balance b/f	42,578
(iv)	Standing orders	3,000	(vii)	Undercast in PDB	900
(vi)	Discount received	27			
	Balance b/f	40,079			
		43,478			43,478

(b) **Reconciliation of the list of balances**

			$	$
(i)		Payables balances per list of balances		44,833
Add:	(iii)	Incorrect balance ($2,597 – $2,579)		18
				44,857
Less:	(ii)	Credit note	372	
	(iv)	Standing order payments	3,000	
	(v)	Debit balance included as a credit balance ($700 × 2)	1,400	4,772
				$40,079

35 JUDITH KELLY – CORRECTING THE RECEIVABLES LEDGER CONTROL ACCOUNT

(a)

Receivables ledger control account

		$			$
(ii)	Balance b/f	120,539	(iv)	Goods returned	2,648
			(vi)	Written off	10
			(viii)	Irrecoverable debt written off	750
				Balance c/d	117,131
		120,539			120,539

(b) **Adjustments to list of personal balances**

(Item)	Increase/(Decrease)	$
(i)	List of personal account balances	122,409
(iii)	Correction of transposition $5,740 should be $7,540	1,800
(v)	Reverse credit balance shown as debit balance = $3,289 × 2	(6,578)
(vii)	Include credit balance omitted	(500)
	Total of personal account balances	117,131

36   JANE MARSHALL – LEDGER ACCOUNTS AND TRIAL BALANCE

Workings:

Cash and bank account

	$		$
Capital	6,200	Rent	180
Sales	52	Wages	56
Receivables	215	Purchases	66
Loan	1,000	Payables	237
		Drawings	100
		Bal c/d	6,828
	7,467		7,467

Capital account

	$		$
Bal c/d	6,200	Cash and bank	6,200
	6,200		6,200

Sales account

	$		$
		Receivables	441
		Receivables	118
		Cash	52
Bal c/d	708	Receivables	97
	708		708

Receivables account

	$		$
Sales	441	Cash and bank	215
Sales	118		
Sales	97	Bal c/d	441
	656		656

Purchases account

	$		$
Payables	237		
Payables	162		
Cash and bank	66	Bal c/d	465
	465		465

Payables account

	$		$
Cash	237	Purchases	237
Bal c/d	162	Purchases	162
	399		399

Rent account

	$		$
Cash and bank	180	Bal c/d	180
	180		180

Wages account

	$		$
Cash and bank	56	Bal c/d	56
	56		56

Drawings account

	$		$
Cash and bank	100	Bal c/d	100
	100		100

Loan account

	$		$
Bal c/d	1,000	Cash and bank	1,000
	1,000		1,000

Trial balance as at...

	$	$
Cash and bank	6,828	
Capital		6,200
Sales		708
Receivables	441	
Purchases	465	
Payables		162
Rent	180	
Wages	56	
Drawings	100	
Loan		1,000
	8,070	8,070

37   K MOLE – ERRORS IN THE BOOKS

(a)   This is an error of **commission**. It must be corrected by debiting **J Mole** and crediting **K Mole**.

(b)   This is an error of **omission**. If an invoice has been omitted completely from the sales day book then it will appear nowhere in the accounting records. This means that in the nominal ledger both **sales** and **receivables** will be understated. In the receivables ledger R Fisher's account balance will also be too small as the invoice will not have been entered into his individual account.

(c)   If the sales tax column of the sales day book has been overcast by $1,000 then the sales tax account will have been **credited** with $1,000 too much and the balance on the sales tax account will therefore be **overstated** by that amount. There will be no effect on the **individual receivables** accounts as the error is one affecting the day book totals only.

(d)   If the discount received column has been undercast by $10 then the double entry posting in the **nominal** ledger for discounts received will be $10 too small. This means that the balance on the discount received account will be $10 too small and the remaining balance on the payables ledger control account will be $10 too **large**. There will be no effect on the individual payables accounts as the error is one concerning totals to the nominal ledger only.

(e)   In this case the invoice has been entered into the sales day book at an amount of $18 greater than its correct value. This will mean that the postings to the nominal ledger are $18 too great. Therefore the **sales** account balance and **receivables ledger** control account balance will both be **overstated** by $18. The incorrect figure of $153 would also have been used to post the individual receivable account for T Toad. Therefore the balance on T Toad's individual account will also be $18 too great.

(f)   The posting of $100 to sales in the nominal ledger will be **correct**. The omission of the sales tax should be corrected by **debiting** the receivables ledger control account and **crediting** the sales tax account. The individual account for S Waterrat should also show the gross total of $117.50.

38 ERROR CORRECTION – JOURNAL

	Date		Details	Dr $	Cr $
(a)	3/3/X5		**P James**	145.79	
			P Jones		145.79
(b)	3/3/X5		Receivables ledger control	**282.00**	
			Sales tax		**42.00**
			Sales		**240.00**
(c)	3/3/X5		Sales	**9.00**	
			Receivables ledger control		**9.00**
(d)	3/3/X5		G Fletcher – **payables** ledger account	250.00	
			G Fletcher – **receivables** ledger account		250.00
			Payables ledger control	250.00	
			Receivables ledger control		250.00
(e)	3/3/X5		**Irrecoverable debt expense**	269.47	
			Receivables ledger control		269.47

39 ERASMUS – SUSPENSE ACCOUNT

(a)

Suspense account

		$			$
(4)	Purchases (357,200 – 345,000)	**12,200**		Balance b/d	7,510
			(3)	Sundry expenses (860 + 860)	**1,720**
			(5)	Cash (4,360 – 3,460)	**900**
			(5)	Sales revenue (6,430 – 4,360)	**2,070**
		12,200			**12,200**

(b) *Errors*

(1) As the entry has not been made, this is an error of **omission**.

(2) This is an error of **commission**. An expense account has been debited, but it is the wrong expense account.

Section 4

ANSWERS TO MULTIPLE-CHOICE QUESTIONS

BUSINESS TRANSACTIONS AND DOCUMENTATION

1   A

Selling provides profit for organisations and credit sales normally occur frequently. Payments to suppliers tend to be carried out once or twice a month. Employees are paid weekly and/or monthly and equipment purchases are infrequent.

2   B

Many business transactions are on credit terms or are settled by cheque. However, some small transactions, such as for local purchases of stationery, are best made by cash. The petty cash system is used in these circumstances.

3   D

A credit note is issued in respect of returned or damaged goods. In these circumstances the amount the customer needs to pay must be reduced. The credit note identifies the amount of the reduction.

4   B

The delivery note is sent with the goods to the customer. It lists the contents of the delivery. The other items are used internally for accounting and other purposes.

5   A

The remittance advice accompanies the cheque to settle an outstanding amount.

6   A

The purchase invoice is received from the supplier and indicates the amount owed for goods or services supplied. It will detail the product supplied and contain sales tax details.

7   B

The goods received note is an internal document which contains the details of the delivery note but in a standard form used within the business accepting the goods. The next stage is to be charged for the goods and the amount to be paid is detailed on the invoice. The statement follows the invoices and credit notes for the month. The advice note indicates the goods are coming and arrives before the delivery note.

8   C

Keith is the purchaser who is being advised of the amount he needs to pay by the invoice from the supplier. Once he has paid, he may be sent a receipt to acknowledge payment. A credit note would arise if there was a problem with the paper and Keith returned all or part of it. A goods received note is an internal record of goods delivered.

9   D

The petty cash voucher acts as a source document for petty cash transactions. It is signed by the person making the payment or asking for reimbursement and is commonly authorised by an appropriate person in the organisation. Evidence of the expenditure (such as a till receipt, a rail or bus ticket) is often stapled to the voucher. An invoice is used for credit transactions but not petty cash. Money should not be borrowed from petty cash so no IOU should appear in the petty cash records.

10   B

A paying in slip records the amount paid into the bank account and acts as a source document for the cash book. Delivery notes and goods received notes details amounts of products and not financial details so are not source documents. A statement is confirmation of transactions and includes details of source documents.

11   D

Once the cheque requisition has been authorised a cheque may be sent. The cheque will be sent with a remittance advice. Debit and credit notes are used to indicate an under or overcast on an invoice, for example.

12   B

The payslip indicates the gross and net pay of an employee as well as detailing any deductions for tax, national insurance and other adjustments to wages and salaries. An advice slip is used to advise a customer that goods/services are due to be delivered. A purchase order may be placed with a supplier to order goods/services, but not with an employee. A quotation is an indication of the cost of a job.

13   C

Invoices tend to generally be headed 'Invoice'. They are a purchase invoice to a customer and sales invoice to the supplier. Credit and debit notes are specific documents used to correct errors, for example. A receipt is given by a supplier to a customer to indicate payment has been made.

14   C

Tax law requires businesses to keep records of purchases, sales, payments to employees, and so on, for a number of years in case there is a need to investigate the affairs of the organisation. Some documents may be kept because a business wishes to build an historic record of its progress but there is no requirement for this to take place. Past performance may or may not help with forecasting, but keeping documents for planning is not a requirement.

15   C

Data protection legislation is designed to protect the individual against information being kept for other than legitimate reasons. Certain information kept about employees for tax purposes, for example, is legitimately kept. Any information recorded about individuals is subject to data protection and other legislation.

16   D

Personal data maintained for domestic purposes is excluded as data protection laws typically apply to businesses. This may include contact details and other personal information relating to friends and family. Personal data of customer and suppliers who are 'natural persons' rather than corporate bodies, is also covered by typical data protection law.

DOUBLE ENTRY BOOKKEEPING

17   B

Horace introduced $5,000 into the business and as a result cash at bank (an asset) is increased. The cash account has the debit entry (increase in asset). The capital account has the credit entry, since increases in capital are always credited to the capital account.

18   C

As in the previous question, this is a transaction that records an increase in assets (car account) and an increase in capital.

19   C

The $900 is a debit balance because the total value of debit entries ($1,750) exceeds the total value of credits ($850). The balance b/d is therefore a debit balance.

20   C

An increase in capital and an increase in liability both require credit entries in the appropriate accounts. Debits and credits must match each other.

21   D

The accounting equation is Assets = Capital + Liabilities. So, we can have:

Assets ($14,000) = Capital ($10,000) + Liabilities ($4,000)

22   D

Receipts in the cash book are always debits. As a receivable account exists from selling on credit, the receivable is credited to complete the double entry.

23   B

	$
Closing capital	4,500
Opening capital	(10,000)
Decrease in net assets	(5,500)
Drawings: profit taken out	8,000
Capital introduced	(4,000)
Loss for the year	(1,500)

24   C

Payments appear on the credit side of the cash book, so the double entry representing the expense settled or asset purchased is a debit.

25   D

The motor van account is used to record this capital expenditure. The supplier is an account payable to the organisation until the amount outstanding is paid.

26   A

When the cash or bank account is reduced, it is credited in the accounts of the business. Drawings are, therefore, debited.

27   B

The inventory account only alters at the end of the year when an inventory take occurs and inventory is valued. When inventory is bought, is the cost is debited to the purchases account. When it is sold, the sale is credited to the sales account. Receipts are recorded on the debit side of the cash book.

28   C

Electricity is an expense. Assets and expenses accounts have debit balances. The remainder are examples of income and liabilities which have credit balances.

29   D

Trade payables are short-term liabilities. All liabilities have credit balances. The other items are drawings, an expense and an asset, all of which have debit balances.

30   A

A receipt in cash is a debit to the cash book. When the customer is sold goods on credit, this creates an account receivable balance. So when the receivable pays the amount outstanding, the account receivable account is credited.

31   C

The separate entity principle relates to the business and its owner. Separate entity recognises the difference between them. A and B focus on different aspects of the accounts but are within the business. There is a clear separation between owner of a business and a lender.

32   C

A bank overdraft is a liability as technically it is repayable whenever the bank demands. Accounts receivables and inventories are assets, and drawings represent a withdrawal of capital.

33   A

Petty cash, the salesman's motor car and computer software are all examples of assets. The owner is a liability representing the amount the business owes its owner.

34   D

This is a variation on the conventional accounting equation. Opening capital plus profit less drawings is the closing capital after a period of trading.

35   A

Drawings represent cash and goods withdrawn. Withdrawals by an owner are not classified as an expense, to prevent manipulation of profit by the owner. Inventory represents goods held for resale. A liability is an amount owed by the business.

36   D

The assets of the business are separate from those of the owner.

37   A

A purchase of inventory on credit increases assets and liabilities. There is an equal effect on current assets and current liabilities, so net assets remain the same. Capital is not affected until the inventory is sold for a profit or loss. Then, at that stage, the capital will change.

38   B

Cash, an asset, decreases. Expenses are charged against income, thus reducing profit.

39 B

The general ledger contains the accounts which are not specific personal accounts for customers and suppliers. It is not a book of original entry (although, in computerised systems, details from source documents are often posted straight to the ledger without the use of books of prime entry). Details of non-current assets are maintained in the non-current asset register.

40 C

The payables ledger contains the accounts of all suppliers. Customer accounts are held in the receivables ledger. Details of credit limits and personal details are not necessarily maintained in the payables ledger. However, in computerised accounting systems it is customary to record such information when setting up the ledger account for the supplier in the records.

41 B

Income and capital have credit balances. Expenses and drawings, together with assets, have debit balances.

42 B

Source documents are entered into books of prime or original entry in manual accounting systems before being posted to the ledger. Ledger accounts include all the double-entry accounts.

43 A

Ledger accounts are posted using the entries in the books of prime entry. The other books and the journal take transactions directly from the source documents.

44 A

Anything which represents a purchase of a non-current asset or which significantly improves a non-current asset is an example of capital expenditure. Day-to-day expenditure, which will be used up within a year, is revenue expenditure.

45 C

(i), (ii) and (iv) will all last for a period longer than a year and represent investment by the business in non-current assets and capital expenditure. Repairs simply keep the computer going and are revenue expenditure.

46 C

(ii), (iii) and (iv) are running expenses needed to operate the business day to day and are revenue expenditure. The purchase of a delivery van represents capital expenditure on a non-current asset to be used in the organisation for some years.

47   A

The cost of a non-current asset includes expenses required in its purchase, such as legal costs, installation costs and so on. All of these are capital expenditure. Rent and repairs are revenue expenditure on day-to-day business expenses. Introducing capital is not expenditure.

48   D

The chairs are inventory and will not remain in the business for very long. The delivery van and office building are long lasting and capital expenditure. Tax is an amount owed to a government body and does not represent day-to-day or long-term expenditure for the business itself. It is classed as an appropriation of profit.

49   A

The bank deposit account is an asset. The bank overdraft and lank loan represent examples of liabilities. The capital account represents an amount due by the business to the proprietor, although it is not regarded as a business liability.

50   A

Capital is a liability and not expenditure.

51   B

The account is balanced by introducing a credit transaction (balance c/d) and the double entry is a debit balance b/d. This ensures the balance remains as a debit balance.

52   A

The account is balanced by introducing a debit transaction (balance c/d) and the double entry is a credit balance b/d. This ensures the balance remains as a credit balance.

53   B

Cash is an asset and a bank overdraft is a liability, so the cash balance will be a debit and the bank overdraft a credit.

54   D

Equipment

	$		$
Balance b/d	1,000	Bank (disposal/sale)	800
Bank (purchase)	1,000	Balance c/d	1,200
	———		———
	2,000		2,000
	———		———
Balance b/d	1,200		

55   C

Machinery

	$		$
Balance b/d	2,000	Bank (disposal/sale)	1,800
Bank (purchase)	2,000	Balance c/d	2,200
	———		———
	4,000		4,000
	———		———
Balance b/d	2,200		

56   B

	$
Opening capital	20,000
Capital introduced	4,000
	———
	24,000
Drawings: profit taken out	(15,000)
	———
	9,000
Profit for the year (bal fig)	14,000
	———
Closing capital	23,000
	———

57   B

Assets and expenses are debit items. Income and liabilities are credit items.

58   B

This double entry correctly records an asset purchased and reduction of the cash account.

59   C

This double entry correctly records an increase in the cash account and an increase in the ownership interest.

60   D

This double entry correctly records a reduction in the liability to the supplier and a reduction in the cash account.

61   C

Drawing and capital introduced represent transactions between the proprietor and the business. Inventory is an asset.

62 D

Computer equipment, petty cash balance and office photocopier are examples of assets. Computer maintenance is an expense.

63 D

Opening capital + profit - drawings = Closing capital. The accounting equation states that proprietor's capital = net assets. Therefore, closing net assets = closing capital.

64 B

The purchase of a car for the business, whether it is new or second-hand, is an example of capital expenditure. Repairs and insurances costs are examples of expenses.

65 C

The purchase of the printer is an example of capital expenditure. All other items are examples of revenue expenditure.

66 B

The purchase of a delivery van represents capital expenditure as the van would be expected to be used in the business for a number of years. Painting and decoration of the office is an example of revenue expenditure.

BANKING AND PETTY CASH

67 C

Using supplier name only may still create inefficiencies when trying to locate individual invoices if the supplier in question is a major supplier of the organisation. Similarly, using purchase invoice date only is likely to be inefficient if there are lots of purchase invoices with the same date. Each supplier will have its own sales invoice sequential order or reference system (i.e. the purchase invoice number from your perspective) – again, not a sensible method of filing and retaining purchase invoices Using both supplier name in alphabetical order and invoice date will be the most effective filing method.

68 A

All of the options stated are disadvantages of not having a document retention policy.

69 B

Many organisations operate a single sequential order filing system for sales invoices. This enables individual sales invoices to be located relatively easily. The other options available lack precision as a system of filing and are therefore relatively inefficient.

70   C

The value of a sale may be recorded on a sales order or a sales invoice. Confirmation that goods have been received will be recorded on a delivery note received from the supplier at the time of delivery. Evidence of payment will be recorded in the cash book and on a remittance advice. A purchase requisition will record the nature and quantity of goods required, and signed by a responsible person to confirm that they are a required for a valid business purpose.

71   D

All four options are advantages of having a document retention policy.

72   B

Cash at bank account

	$		$
Cash sales	900	Balance b/d	500
		Balance c/d	400
	——		——
	900		900
	——		——
Balance b/d	400		

73   B

Payment is due in the future so this is a credit transaction and not a cash transaction. The other options are all immediate and involve cash or bank, so are cash transactions.

74   D

A remittance advice provides information of what the payment constitutes e.g. which invoices have been paid. It is not the payment itself.

75   A

The drawer is the person signing the cheque. The drawee is the bank on which the cheque is drawn. The payee is the person to whom the cheque is made out. The payer is not a term used in the legalities associated with cheques.

76   A

An endorsement (signing the cheque on the reverse) is a way of enabling a cheque, not crossed 'account payee only', to be placed in someone else's account. Crossing a cheque limits the use of the cheque. Although it can be endorsed, it should be paid into a bank account rather than being cashed. A cheque guarantee is available up to the limit of a cheque guarantee card, but this is only available between the drawer and the payee and not a third party. A credit transfer is another form of transferring money through the banking system.

77   C

A charge card (e.g. American Express, Diners Club) balance must be paid off in full. Unlike credit cards, no credit facilities are offered. A debit card allows the customer to make payment of a bill electronically from his/her bank account. A cheque guarantee card 'guarantees' a cheque up to the limit of the card, as long as its conditions have been met.

78   D

The amount of a direct debit can be varied and is originated by the recipient (i.e. the company operating the store card in this case). The other forms of transfer are all originated by the bank customer. The standing order is for a fixed amount, until it is changed. Credit and mail transfers are not automatic.

79   D

The drawee is the bank of the person who is making the payment. The person or business paying and signing the cheque is the drawer. The person or business paid is the payee.

80   C

Crossing the cheque means that the cheque cannot be cashed. It must be paid into a bank account. If crossed 'account payee' it must be paid into the account of the payee and no one else.

81   A

Immediate settlement of a debt is possible using a debit card. Payment by a credit card or charge card is from a separate account, which the customer will need to pay off at a later date. Cheques are not immediate.

82   A

The amount of a direct debit can be varied and is originated by the recipient (the utility company in this case). An inter-bank transfer tends to be used for larger amounts, such as the settlement of house purchases. It is not a regular arrangement. A standing order is for a fixed amount, until it is changed. EFTPOS is the name of an electronic transfer systems used for BACS payroll payments to employees, for example.

83   C

A remittance advice details the amount paid. This may be the total of a statement received from a supplier, or simply part of that total. A debit note may be issued if, for example, an invoice is undercast in error. A remittance list accompanies and lists the cheques paid into the bank.

84   B

The originator of the direct debit is able to vary the amount of the direct debit charge each time payment is requested. This is suitable for paying monthly heat and light charges as usage and charges are likely to vary each month. The direct debit authorisation will not contain a specific or fixed amount to be paid.

85   B

The drawer of a cheque is the account holder whose account will be debited when the cheque is presented for payment. The person who is the recipient of the cheque is the payee and the bank in which the cheque is drawn is the drawee.

86   B

The cheque card guarantees cheques up to the limit defined on the cheque guarantee card so long as certain conditions are fulfilled. All the other options offer the facility to make payments directly without the need for a cheque.

87   B

Companies other than banks may issue credit cards. It is important that the retailer accepting the credit card checks that the card is valid and belongs, as far as can be seen, to the person presenting it. These security measures militate against fraud.

88   D

It is a relatively short time in the UK. Because of geographical and other difficulties in other countries it can take longer. More automated and electronic systems can speed up the system.

89   A

Because banks provide a variety of services for customers, all of these relationships are relevant. The main relationship is receivable/payable, because one party always owes the other. The bank acts as agent for the customer when making payment on the customer's behalf. Mortgagor/mortgagee may arise when borrowing. Bailment arises when the bank holds securities and other valuables for the customer, say, in the bank vaults.

90   B

Restoration of the imprest means putting the petty cash balance back to the imprest amount. So, assuming there is no income during the period, the amount of cash needed will equal the total of the vouchers.

91   C

The bank provides useful services for the customer, so the customer has to take a degree of care in operating his/her account. The customer is not a salesperson for the bank and there is no reason why a customer should not have more than one account with more than one bank.

92   D

There is less in the till than there should be, because there would have been $250 in the till at the start of the day. According to the cash register, there should have been $1,323.21 in the till at the end of the day.

93   **C**

A crossed cheque must be paid into a bank account. The further restriction is that the crossing is stated to be "Account payee" which means that it can only be paid into the bank account of the payee, A Smith.

94   **D**

This ensures that the correct amount is charged to petty cash and the entertainment account.

95   **B**

All of these represent the items needed to make a payment into the bank. A cheque remittance list may also be used, but it is not a requirement.

96   **C**

There is no difference because there is a compensating error in both cash and the petty cash records. All the other options lead to a difference in either the cash or the vouchers.

97   **C**

	$
Sales	193.24
Less: wages	(20.00)
	173.24

98   **C**

Petty cash is used for small items and for convenience. Larger items, particularly when invoiced, would normally go through the usual channels and be paid by cheque.

99   **B**

	$
Opening balance	65
Less: payments	(64)
Add: replenished from bank	50
	51

100   **C**

Although the petty cash is a relatively small amount in comparison with the overall transactions of a business, it should still be held securely.

101 C

It saves invoicing or making out cheques for small amounts.

102 C

The proof of expenditure is linked to receipts and other information received about payments made.

103 D

Any cheque more than six months old may be returned by the customer's bank, so the quickest and most appropriate action is to contact the customer to alter the cheque. 'Correcting' the date could be regarded as fraud. Banks write 'refer to drawer' on cheques when returning them. The supplier would not do this.

104 D

BACS involves electronic payments through the banking system and is suitable for payroll.

105 A

The transactions by cheque, direct debit, standing order and other bank transactions are shown on a bank statement. A statement records the transactions between customer and supplier. Petty cash transactions are included in the petty cash book, but there is no external source of information about the transactions. Statements of the transactions on a company credit card are supplied by the card issuer.

106 A

The checkout operator has no authorisation to grant credit and allow the customer to return later. Neither has the operator the ability to change the limit on a debit card. Having the customer arrested is rather drastic. This could result in bad publicity for the supermarket, especially if a mistake has been made.

107 C

A credit card in excess of its limit and an incorrectly completed cheque are invalid as methods of payment. Barter is a way of swapping one item for another and is only useful in limited circumstances. Cash is always acceptable.

108 B

Authorisation requires evidence and a correctly authorised form requiring a cheque to be sent to the supplier. A receipt would not be seen until after payment has been made and a remittance advice is not drawn up until after the cheque is ready to be sent. At the stage the cheque is drawn, the amount in the bank would not be a major consideration. This would or should have been arranged by senior managers.

109 B

Words, figures, date, drawer and payee details should be correct assuming the input is correct. However, if incorrect details have been input to the accounting package and insufficient controls exist in the business, fraud could occur and cheques could be falsely sent to dummy suppliers whose transactions are fictional. All cheques and forms of payment made by an organisation should be authorised and checked.

110 B

This is a procedure to check the work of cashiers. Regular checks, at unknown intervals, are designed to encourage accuracy and discourage fraud. The correctness of documentation can be assessed elsewhere in the business away from the tills. Performance is also looked at in a more global way, but the 'success' of single tills is generally available by looking at duplicate till rolls or from electronic output generated by modern tills.

111 A

An increase in the petty cash float represents an increase in that asset (a debit) and a reduction in the cash account represents a reduction in that asset (a credit).

112 D

$54 + $36 + $17 - $35 − $20 = $52

113 C

SALES AND SALES RETURNS

114 C

Harper owes the amount of the sale price including sales tax.

$500 + (17.5% × $500) = $587.50

115 $5,300

Sales tax account

	$		$
Payables/bank (input sales tax)	6,000	Balance b/d	3,400
Bank	2,600	Receivables/bank (output sales tax)	10,500
Balance c/d	5,300		
	———		———
	13,900		13,900
	———		———
		Balance b/d	5,300

Sales tax on sales (outputs) = 17.5% × $60,000 = $10,500

Sales tax on purchases (inputs) = (17.5/117.5) × $40,286 = $6,000

116 A

The sales day book is the book of original entry for sales on credit. Sales tax on sales is also first recorded in this book of prime entry in a manual system.

117 A

The credit sale is entered in the sales day book and the cash sale is recorded in the cash book.

118 B

Sales revenue transactions are recorded at values excluding sales tax, as credit entries.

119 C

Cash sales are first recorded in the cash book and sales tax is also first recorded there in a memorandum column.

120 B

The receivable's account should be debited with the full amount payable, including the tax. The entry in the sales account should be for the sales value excluding sales tax. Sales tax payable to the tax authorities should be credited to the sales tax account (liability = credit balance).

121 A

	$
List price	1,325.00
Less: trade discount at 20%	265.00
	————
	1,060.00
	————

Sales tax 10% × $1,060.00 = $106.00

122 B

$12,000 × 90% × 15% = $1,620

123 C

This is a sale for payment at a future date. Immediate sales are cash sales.

124 C

$100 × 95% = $95.00

125 B

$414 × 100/115 = $360 credit to sales

126   D

The sales tax is accounted for at the date of sale. At the time of receipt, it is the total of the invoice that is recorded in the accounts.

127   C

This indicates more sales tax has been paid out than received, so sales tax is recoverable from the tax authorities.

128   D

Accounts receivable

	$		$
Opening balance	4,529	Cash	7,231
Sales $16,540 × 60%	9,924	Balance c/d	7,222
	———		———
	14,453		14,453
	———		———

129   D

Receivables account

	$		$
Opening balance	5,329	Cash (bal fig)	80,138
Sales ($69,200 × 1.15)	79,580	Closing balance	4,771
	———		———
	84,909		84,909
	———		———

130   B

		$	$
June 12	Purchases: list price		5,000
	Less trade discount (25%)		(1,250)
			———
			3,750
June 16	Returns: list price	(1,000)	
	Less trade discount	250	
		———	(750)
			———
			3,000
June 16	Payment (50%)		(1,500)
			———
June 30	Balance owed		1,500
			———

131 B

Settlement discount allowed to a credit customer, when they were not originally expected to take advantage of the discount terms, will be accounted for as a reduction in revenue receivable.

132 C

Victoria pays $240 × 0.175 = $42

Fraser pays $360 × 0.175 − 42 = $21

133 B

Sales tax account				
	$			$
Input tax $18,480 × 10/110	1,680	Opening balance b fwd		3,210
Cash paid	2,890	Output tax $21,700 × 10%		2,170
Closing balance c/fwd	810			
	5,380			5,380

134 A

To reduce overdue balances in the receivables ledger accounts, customers owing money have to be persuaded to pay more quickly. Improved debt collection methods should do this. Allowing credit customers to pay more slowly and giving customers more credit will add to the problems of late payment, not reduce them.

135 B

	$
Sales tax on sales: $1,200 × 20/120	200.00
Less: Sales tax on purchases $810 × 20/120	(135.00)
	65.00

136 B

Output tax represents the sales tax generated from goods and services provided by a business.

137 D

Sales tax account

	$		$
Sales tax on purchases	900	Balance b/d	2,400
Balance c/d	2,750	Sales tax on sales	1,050
		Repayment	200
	_____		_____
	3,650		3,650
	_____		_____
		Balance b/d	2,750

138 D

The consumer, who is unable to reclaim the sales tax, pays the tax.

139 B

Sales tax account

	$		$
Input sales tax ($15,200 × 17½%)	2,660	Output sales tax ($24,600 × 17½%)	4,305
Balance c/d	1,645		
	_____		_____
	4,305		4,305
	_____		_____
		Balance b/d	1,645

140 C

Sales tax account

	$		$
Input tax $30,785 × 17.5/117.5	4,585	Output tax $34,800 × 0.175	6,090
Balance c/d	1,505		
	_____		_____
	6,090		6,090
	_____		_____

141 C

Sales tax account

	$		$
Input sales tax ($54,200 × 0.175)	9,485	Opening balance	1,354
Balance c/d	2,614	Output sales tax ($72,145 × 17.5/	
		117.5)	10,745
	_____		_____
	12,099		12,099
	_____		_____

142 A

The invoice determines the tax point from which sales tax is calculated.

143 C

Registration is determined according to limits set by the government.

144 D

Irrecoverable debts are a product of non-payment and time. The longer a debt is outstanding, the less likely it is to be settled. Matters such as insolvency of the receivable also lead to an irrecoverable debt.

145 C

The sales returns day book is the book of original entry for returns in a manual system. It enables the business to monitor returns more easily than maintaining records for returns together with those for sales.

146 A

An aged receivables analysis lists the amounts and time invoices are outstanding for named receivables. It is a device used in credit control and receivables are contacted and 'chased' for amounts outstanding longer than the agreed credit period.

147 B

Coding involves recording an account number for each account. The numbers or codes are then used to post the source documents to the appropriate accounts.

148 B

An account which becomes an irrecoverable debt is, initially, an account receivable. So to clear the account, a credit is needed to the account receivable. The other part of the double entry is a debit to irrecoverable debts. At the end of an accounting period, the total of irrecoverable debts is then transferred to the statement of comprehensive income.

149 A

Writing off an irrecoverable (bad) debt is an internal measure which usually follows credit control and legal action. Once it is not cost effective to continue action the account is written off, but the organisation will still hope payment is made at some future time. If a statement is sent, this communicates to the receivable that there is no need to pay.

150 C

Accounts receivable have debit balances. The sum is cleared by the goods returned and the bad debt written off.

151 D

Registration is determined according to limits set by the government.

$500 × 1.2 = $600.00 – i.e. $500.00 + $100 sales tax.

152 C

Sales tax account

	$		$
Input tax 64,200 × 20/120	10,700	Opening balance	4,500
Cash paid	3,600	Output tax $80,000 × 0.20	16,000
Closing balance	6,200		
	————		————
	20,500		20,500
	————		————

153 B

	$
List price	1,480.00
Less: trade discount 5%	(74.00)
	————
	1,406.00
Add: sales tax 20%	281.20
	————
	1,687.20

154 D

	$
List price	10,500.00
Less: trade discount 8%	(840.00)
	————
	9,660.00
Add: sales tax 20%	1,932.00
	————
	11,592.00

155 C

The trade receivables account should account for the full (gross) amount due from the customer. This is calculated as follows: $423.00 × 1.20 = $507.60. This is an amount due to the business; it is a debit balance.

156 C

The cash receipts book would analyse the total receipt between the net sale amount and the sales tax associated with that sale.

157 D

	$
List price	14,500.00
Less: trade discount 4%	(580.00)
	13,920.00
Less: cash discount 5%	(696.00)
	13,224.00

PURCHASES AND PURCHASE RETURNS

158 A

Total cost of items purchased, including sales tax = $120 + $60 + $190 = $370.

Sales tax = 17.5/117.5 of this total. $370 × 17.5/117.5 = $55.11.

159 A

The purchase day book records purchase invoices received from suppliers for items purchased on credit. The correct posting is to debit purchases and credit payables. Here, the credit is to the suppliers' accounts in the payables ledger. Answer C has the debit and credit the wrong way round. Answers B and D are incorrect because the Cash book is not affected by the receipt of purchase invoices.

160 C

The purchase return reduces the amount owed to Rawlings by $800 plus sales tax.

$800 + (17.5% × $800) = $940.00

161 B

Purchases are recorded excluding sales tax, provided the business is registered for sales tax.

162 C

The payables ledger control account records transactions in total with the suppliers to the business. The balance on the control account is the total amount owed by the business to all its suppliers.

163 B

Sales tax is chargeable on the price after deducting the trade discount of 20%. The full purchase price is therefore 1.175 × $1,600 = $1,880. Since the trader is not registered for sales tax, the purchases account should be debited with this full amount, including the tax. (A different situation arises when a trader is registered for sales tax.)

164 A

Sales tax on sales = (10/110) × $45,237.50 = $4,112.50

Sales tax on purchases = 10% × $31,500 = $3,150.00

Net amount of sales tax payable (credit balance) = $4,112.50 − $3,150.00 = $962.50

165 A

The payables ledger control account should be debited with the full amount of the purchase return, including the tax. The returns outwards account should be credited with the value of the returns excluding the sales tax. The sales tax account should be credited with the amount of tax on the returns (since the tax is no longer recoverable).

166 B

Paying an account payable reduces cash by the amount of the payment and also reduces the total amounts owed to accounts payable, a current liability.

167 C

Returns outwards are purchase returns to suppliers. They can be thought of as 'negative purchases' or 'negative expense', so we credit a returns outwards account. The returns reduce the amount owed to payables, so we debit the payables account (reducing a liability = debit entry).

168 C

The series of transactions might be recorded as follows.

Original purchase

Debit Purchases and Credit Brad – account payable

On issuing the cheque

Debit Brad – account payable and Credit Bank (cash book)

On cancellation of the cheque

Debit Bank (cash book) and Credit Returns outwards

169 C

The goods are first identified as being needed and then an order is placed. Once the goods are delivered an organisation may find it useful to make out its own form to record the goods. This is the purpose of the goods received note. This would then be followed by an invoice and possibly a statement. Payment would be made accompanied by a remittance advice.

170 B

Purchases returns are recorded from a credit note and not an invoice.

171 D

The sales tax is determined at the time of sale as opposed to the order.

172 D

The inventory account is only used on the valuation of inventory at the end of an accounting period.

Purchases are recorded as a debit, and purchases on credit create accounts payable.

173 D

This indicates the time provided for credit.

174 C

Payables' account

	$		$
Cash	11,583	Opening balance	2,660
Closing balance	3,528	Purchases (bal fig)	12,451
	———		———
	15,111		15,111
	———		———

175 A

Payables' account

	$		$
Cash ($85,460 – $35,640)	49,820	Opening balance	14,550
Closing balance	12,560	Purchases (bal fig)	47,830
	———		———
	62,380		62,380
	———		———

176 D

Accounts payable account

	$		$
Cash (bal fig)	46,289	Opening balance	6,711
Closing balance	6,538	Purchases ($85,400 × 54%)	46,116
	———		———
	52,827		52,827
	———		———

177 B

	Payables account		
	$		$
Cash	29,660	Opening balance (bal fig)	3,819
Closing balance	4,286	Purchases (25,640 × 1.175)	30,127
	———		———
	33,946		33,946
	———		———

178 D

Trade discount is recorded on the invoice and is not brought into the accounts.

179 D

Discounts received reduce the amount a business needs to pay to its supplier.

180 C

The sales invoice is prepared excluding settlement discount as Carling Co is not expected to take advantage of the settlement discount terms. When Carling Co does subsequently pay early, Premier Co must account for the receipt of cash and reduction in revenue receivable in order to clear the receivable originally recorded.

181 B

Maycee Co is the purchaser and will record settlement discount received when it makes payment of the invoice within the appropriate time.

182 C

Purchases and sales tax are debited and Marsh Co credited. The use of codes simply replaces names with numbers.

183 B

The list of payables includes amounts outstanding over time. The time element can be monitored closely to ensure discounts are not missed. As the list is of payables and not receivables, the aged payables analysis is no help in identifying irrecoverable debts.

It is a list of payables which is, in its own right, not a good reason for keeping the aged payables analysis. Other records must be kept to ensure orders are delivered because until an invoice has been issued, an account payable is not created.

184 D

The numbers of invoices would be checked off against the statement and duplicate numbers would be easily spotted. Errors in calculations and discounts should be picked up when checking the invoices against orders. Non-delivery of items would be identified through the use of other records. Any discrepancies and errors would be communicated to the supplier.

185 C

This is a cash transaction as far as the supplier is concerned who receives payment immediately. So, in the accounts of the buyer, the credit card account replaces bank or cash which are normally used in cash transactions.

186 A

As the types of coding errors are not detailed, A is the most appropriate answer. In a computerised system the accounts always balance. Accounting packages require the double entry to be completed or further transactions cannot be posted. It is not illegal for a business to make mistakes.

187 D

The purchases expense account (a debit balance) should exclude sales tax charged by suppliers. The sales tax is accounted for in a separate sales tax account.

188 C

Sales tax imposed on purchases should be debited to the sales tax account so that it can be offset against sales tax charged by the business on sales.

189 B

Purchase returns represent the cost of goods returned to suppliers. Accounts payable is debited (the liability is reduced) to reflect the fact that those goods should not be paid for now that they have been returned.

190 A

	$
List price	800.00
Less: trade discount 5%	(40.00)
	760.00
Less: settlement discount 3.5%	(26.60)
Amount paid	733.40

191 D

The cash payments book would analyse the total payment between the net purchase costs and the sales tax associated with that purchase.

PAYROLL

192 A

When an employee is paid on the basis of his or her output, at a rate for each unit or piece produced, the remuneration method is called piecework.

193 A

	$
Gross wages	9,900
Employer's social security contributions	925
	10,825

Employees' social security contributions and income tax are deductions from gross wages and so are included within the gross wages total of $9,900.

194 C

John – 135 × $1.15 = $155.25, minimum $165.00

Mike – 140 × $1.10 = $154.00

20 × $1.15 = $23.00

15 × $1.20 = $18.00

TOTAL $195.00

195 D

An income tax code is associated purely with income tax. It is provided by the tax authorities to assist in the calculation of the income tax liability on earnings.

196 B

James – 40 × $6.20 =	$248.00	**Jake** – 35 × $7.40 =	$259.00
5 × $9.30 =	$46.50	6 × $11.10 =	$66.60
3 × $12.40 =	$37.20	7 × $14.80 =	$103.60
TOTAL	$331.70	TOTAL	$429.20

197 A

Percy –Basic weekly wage	$240.00	**Peter** – Basic weekly wage	$260.00
Bonus 5%	$12.00	Bonus 5%	$13.00
		Production bonus	$40.00
TOTAL	$252.00	TOTAL	$313.00

198 C

	$
Pay for 1st 200 pallets (200 × $2)	400
Pay for next 35 pallets (35 × $3)	105
Gross pay	505

199 B

The income tax deducted is a liability to the taxation authorities. The employer merely collects this tax on behalf of the taxation authorities and will pay it to them periodically. The gross amount of salaries (i.e. including the income tax deducted) is shown as an expense.

200 B

This is usually paid over during the month following collection. (Note: this may vary between and within countries, for example: small business may remit income tax on a quarterly basis.)

201 B

The gross pay comprises net pay and deductions made against gross pay. The employer pays the total plus state benefit contributions incurred by the employer.

202 D

$$\frac{4}{52} \times \$15{,}000 = \$1{,}153.85$$

203 B

	$
40 hours at $7	280
6 hours at $10.50	63
	343

204 D

	$
Basic commission $90,000 × 2%	1,800
Expensive items $22,000 × 0.5%	110
Sales over $70,000 ($90,000 – $70,000) × 1%	200
	2,110

205 C

	$
38 hours at $7.50	285.00
6 hours at $7.50 × 1.25	56.25
	————
	341.25
	————

206 B

The payroll function is involved in calculating pay. Management or human resources decide matters such as holidays.

207 C

The other information is useful in determining the performance of employees under different headings.

208 C

Third party authorisation is essential as part of the control process in payroll. Only authorised documents confirming work has been completed should be used as evidence that wages and salaries have been earned and need to be paid.

209 D

The payroll documentation gives all details of the basis for the gross pay and all deductions. Any errors here will just be reflected in the payslip. The latter does not provide details of the basic calculations of gross pay. The tax authorities simply hold details about tax and not the breakdown of pay of individual employees. The employee's manager may be aware of the hours an employee worked or the jobs on which he was involved. But the manager is unlikely to be aware of technical pay details, such as deductions for tax and social security

210 B

Drawings are a withdrawal of capital by a business owner. Drawings are not wages or salaries.

CONTROL ACCOUNTS, BANK RECONCILIATIONS AND THE INITIAL TRIAL BALANCE

211 B

The control account, which is a check on the ledger, should be undertaken by someone who is independent from the day-to-day work.

212 B

The control account is a check, not a replacement for individual ledger accounts.

213 C

Ledger accounts record financial transactions in business. They are subject to reconciliation and control.

214 A

Authorisation is a key element of control.

215 A

An entry is required in the cash book for all the correct items in the bank statement that have not yet been recorded in the cash book. These are the items that the business learns about from the bank statement, and should then record in its own accounts, in the cash book. Such items include bank charges (including overdraft interest) and details of dishonoured cheques. They are also likely to include details of credit transfers, standing orders and direct debit payments.

216 B

	$
Cash book balance (debit, therefore cash in the bank)	25,000
Items not yet in the bank statement:	
Payments to suppliers	3,500
Payments into the account (lodgements)	(3,800)
	———
Bank statement balance	24,700
	———

217 B

	$
Opening balance	(89.93)
Interest	(16.45)
	———
	(106.38)
	———

218 C

	$
Overdraft per bank statement	(38,600)
Deposits not yet credited to the account	41,200
	———
	2,600
Cheques paid but not yet presented to the bank	(3,300)
	———
Overdraft in cash book	(700)
	———

219 D

The cash book should be adjusted for items such as standing order payments and bank charges which have not already been entered in the cash book. The other items feature in the bank reconciliation statement itself.

220 C

A credit in the bank statement is a debit entry in the cash book.

221 C

	$
Cash book balance	148
Bank charges	(10)
Standing order	(25)
Corrected cash book	113

	$
Cash book figure	113
Unpresented cheques	125
Outstanding lodgements	(85)
	153

222 A

	$
Balance per bank statement	(210)
Less: unpresented cheques	(83)
Add: uncredited lodgements	30
Corrected balance per cash book	(263)

223 A

Timing differences between entries being recorded in the cash book until the transactions appear on the bank statement are common.

224 A

Cash book

	$		$
Balance b/d	850	Cheques written	1,200
Sales (cash)	230	Balance c/d	1,380
Receivables (remittances)	1,500		
	2,580		2,580

225 B

	$	$
Balance per bank statement at 1 April		950
Bank statement movements during April Cheques	(1,600)	
Deposits	1,900	
		300
Unpresented cheques at 30 April		(210)
Balance per cash book at 30 April		1,040

Only the reconciling items at 30 April are relevant in this calculation: any reconciling items at 1 April not included in the 30 April items will have passed through the cash book in April.

226 D

Uncredited lodgements are not errors. They result from a timing difference between the recording of receipts in the cash book and their appearance on the bank statement. The latter will occur later, so the bank statement will be 'out of date' compared with the cash book.

227 C

Large amounts of cash and numerous transactions could easily lead to errors. Regular, frequent reconciliations are essential.

228 B

Discounts would not appear on a bank statement, neither would they affect the balance in the cash book.

229 B

Cash would be withdrawn from the bank the same day the cheque has been requisitioned and posted to the cash book. The other instances would require time for the cheque to be presented to the drawee bank.

230 A

The running balance should be recorded on the latest counterfoil whenever a transaction occurs affecting the bank statement. The business owner will then instantly know how much is available in the bank.

231 C

Bank charges may be unknown to the business until charges are placed to the business bank account. The business owner would be advised by letter or simply receipt of the bank statement.

232 A

A credit card purchase is recorded on a credit card statement. The others reflect relatively modern transfers which appear directly on the bank statement.

233 C

The balance on the control account and the total of individual customer balances in the receivables ledger should be the same. They show how much is owed to the business by its credit customers. Here, the receivables ledger balances are $150 less than the control account balance. A receipt has therefore been recorded in the receivables ledger that has not been recorded in the control account. The answer is therefore C.

234 D

Accounts receivable control account reconciliations are carried out to check that the balance on the receivables control account equals the total of all the balances on the individual accounts receivable accounts in the receivables ledger. If a transaction has been posted to the account of the wrong customer in the accounts receivable ledger, the total of receivables balances is not affected. This error would not be discovered by the control account reconciliation.

235 A

Receivables account

	$		$
Opening balance b/d	32,750		
Sales	125,000	Bank	122,500
		Payables contra	550
		Sales returns	1,300
		Closing balance	33,400
	————		————
	157,750		157,750
	————		————
Closing balance	33,400		

236 D

Receivables ledger control account

	$		$
Opening balance	1,586		
SDB	100		
CB	100	Bal c/d	1,786
	————		————
	1,786		1,786
	————		————

237 D

	$
Receivables ledger total balances	50,000
Credit transfer (reduces receivables)	(750)
Contra entry (reduces receivables)	(2,000)
Adjusted receivables ledger balances	47,250

238 A

Receivables control account

	$		$
Balance b/d	8,450	Cheques	22,430
Sales	19,600	Sales returns	1,000
		Contra	540
		Balance c/d	4,080
	28,050		28,050

239 B

Accounts receivable control account

	$		$
Balance b/d	500	Credit notes	170
Sales invoices	1,900	Cash (bal fig)	1,530
		Balance c/d	700
	2,400		2,400

240 D

Trade receivables

	$		$
Balance b/d	54,550	Cash received re credit sales	81,622
Credit sales (bal fig)	81,632	Irrecoverable receivable w/off	2,000
		Balance c/d	52,560
	136,182		136,182

241 B

Assets and expenses		Income, liabilities and capital	
	$		$
Cost of sales	458,000	Sales	628,000
General overheads	138,000	Payables	54,000
Cash on deposit	61,000	Capital	86,000
	657,000		768,000
Therefore receivables	111,000		
	768,000		

The amount for receivables must make the total debits and credits equal.

242 C

A debit balance (amount receivable) has been wrongly treated as a credit balance (amount payable). To correct the error, the payables ledger listing should be reduced by a total of $500 as the error had the effect of overstating the list of balances i.e. need to remove the credit balance and then recognise the debit balance.

243 A

Payables ledger control account

	$		$
CB (14,576 – 14,756)	180	Opening bal	3,446
Receivables ledger control account	392		
Closing bal	2,874		
	3,446		3,446

244 D

Trade payables

	$		$
Cash paid re credit purchases	69,500	Balance b/d	23,450
Balance c/d	25,600	Purchases (bal fig)	71,650
	95,100		95,100

245 B

BNO apparently owes ANO $150 more than the supplier statement identifies. With items, A, C and D the result would be that the supplier will state that you owe more, not less. Item B is the only possible answer which could explain the situation.

246 C

Trade payables' ledger control account

	$		$
Goods returned	1,300	Opening bal	32,750
Cash paid	122,500	Purchases	125,000
Contra with TRC	1,100		
Closing bal	32,850		
	————		————
	157,750		157,750
	————		————

247 B

Trade payables' ledger control account

	$		$
Goods returned	6,500	Opening bal	52,750
Cash paid	322,500	Purchases	325,000
Discount received	5,250		
Closing bal	43,500		
	————		————
	377,750		377,750
	————		————

248 D

Trade payables' ledger control account

	$		$
Goods returned	4,500	Opening bal	34,560
Cash paid	260,000	Purchases	270,000
Discount received	7,500		
Closing bal	32,560		
	————		————
	304,560		304,560
	————		————

249 A

Trade payables' ledger control account

	$		$
Goods returned	3,500	Opening bal	55,555
Cash paid	390,000	Purchases	395,000
Discount received	6,500		
Closing bal	50,555		
	————		————
	450,555		450,555
	————		————

250 A

Trade payables' ledger control account

	$		$
Goods returned	2,500	Opening bal	33,250
Cash paid	335,500	Purchases	339,850
Discount received	3,350		
Closing bal	31,750		
	———		———
	373,100		373,100
	———		———

251 C

Extracting a trial balance identifies the existence of errors that lead to a difference between total debit balances and total credit balances. The answer is therefore C.

Answer D is not correct. An expense item is a debit entry in an expense account, and an entry in a non-current asset account is also a debit entry. Although there is an error, it would not be revealed by a trial balance. Similarly, with answers A and B, the errors leave total debits and total credits the same.

252 A

As a result of the error, total payables are under-stated by $259,440 − $254,940 = $4,500. To correct the error, we need to increase the balance in the payables' ledger control account, and this is done by crediting the control account.

The error has affected the control account only and not the entries in the individual payable account for Figgins Co in the payables ledger control account, so the total of payables' balances is unaffected.

253 D

To correct the error, we need to reduce building repairs expenses (so credit Building repairs account) and we need to record the expense as an increase in equipment repairs costs (so debit the Equipment repairs account). Answer A contains the correct double entry, but describes the transaction as an error of omission. An error of omission is one where no double entry was originally made.

254 B

To correct the error, we need to reduce stationery expenses (so credit Stationery expense account) and we need to record the expense as an increase in advertising costs (so debit the Advertising expense account

255 B

Item B   Discounts received should be a credit balance. Therefore there is no error to correct.

Item A   This is an error where a debit entry has been incorrectly recorded as a credit balance.

Item C If the irrecoverable debt has been omitted entirely, and no accounting entry has been made, there can be no suspense account entry. Here, it would seem that the receivable balance has been reduced for the irrecoverable debt (credit account receivable) but the irrecoverable debt expense account has not recorded the irrecoverable debt. If so, credits exceed debits and a suspense account entry is needed.

Item D The error in item D makes total debits higher by $180. These will therefore cause an entry in the suspense account.

256 B

A suspense account is needed when, as a result of an accounting error, total credit balances and debit balances will not be equal to each other.

Error 1. The entry should have been Credit Bank, Debt Motor Vehicles account. Instead, it was recorded as Credit Bank, Credit Motor Vehicles account. A suspense account is needed.

Error 2. The entry should have been Debit Bank, Credit Brown, but was recorded as Debit Bank, Credit Green. Total credits and debits will be equal, so a suspense account is not needed to correct the error.

Error 3. The entry has been recorded as: Credit Bank $9,500, Debit Rent $5,900. Credits and debits are unequal, so a suspense account is needed.

Error 4. The transaction has been recorded as Credit Receivables, Debit Purchases, but should have been recorded as Credit Receivables, Debit Irrecoverable debts account. Total credits and debits are equal. A suspense account is not required to correct the error.

Error 5. An omission of a transaction does not need a suspense account to correct it.

257 B

Assets		*Liabilities and capital*	
	$		$
Purchases	16,000	Sales	43,000
Equipment	22,000	Overdraft	8,000
Inventory	19,000	Capital	6,000
	57,000		57,000

258 D

Discounts received should be recorded as:

Debit Payables ledger control account, and Credit Discounts received.

Here, the discount has been debited instead of credited, so that the balance in the discounts received account is 2 × $200 = $400 too low. To correct, we must:

Credit Discounts received $400, and Debit Suspense account $400.

259 C

Since total debits are less than total credits in the trial balance by ($1,026,480 – $992,640) $33,840, we need a debit balance of $33,840 in the suspense account to make the total debits and total credits equal.

Error 1. Does not affect the suspense account, because it is an omission and omissions do not alter debits and credits.

Error 2. Has treated a debit balance of $27,680 as a credit balance, as a result of which total credits will exceed total debits by 2 × $27,680 = $55,360.

Error 3. Does not affect the suspense account since there is a debit and matching credit.

Error 4. Has been to omit a credit balance of $21,520 for rent payable, as a result of which total debits will exceed total credits by $21,520.

To correct the errors:	$
Credit suspense account	55,360
Debit suspense account	21,520
	———
To eliminate suspense account balance	33,840
	———

260 C

A suspense account is needed when, as a result of an accounting error, total credit balances and debit balances will not be equal to each other.

Error 1. When the cash refund is paid, the entry should be Credit Cash, Debit Receivables ledger control account. There are two errors to consider. First, there has only been one entry in the general ledger (there has been no entry to the Receivables ledger control account and this would create a suspense account. The second error is that the wrong customer account has been used, and a debit entry has been recorded as a credit entry.

Error 5. The entry should have been Credit Bank, Debit Plant repairs, but has been Credit Bank, Credit Plant and equipment account. A suspense account is needed to correct this error.

Errors 2, 3 and 4 do not result in total debits and total credits being unequal.

Error 2. The wrong accounts have been used, but the debit entry and credit entry are equal. (The correct entry should be Credit Purchases, Debit Drawings, with the cost of the goods withdrawn.)

Error 3. The accounting entries made were Debit Accounts Payable, Credit Sales, but should have been Debit Accounts Payable, Credit Accounts Receivable. However, the total debits and total credits posted to the nominal ledger are equal.

Error 4. Presumably, these transactions have been omitted from the accounts entirely.

261 A

Think of the other side of the double entry that is needed to correct the error. This will help you to decide whether the entry in the suspense account should be a debit or a credit entry.

Error 1. To correct, we must debit gas account $180, therefore credit suspense account.

Error 2. To correct, we need to remove the credit to the Payables ledger control account of $50 and then debit it with $50. The correction therefore requires a credit the suspense account with 2 × $50.

Error 3. To correct, we need to credit interest receivable, therefore we debit suspense account.

Suspense account

	$		$
Balance (balancing figure)	210	Gas expense	180
Interest received	70	Payables ledger control	100
	——		——
	280		280
	——		——

262 C

The error you should look for is one where the correction will require:

Debit: Suspense account, and Credit: the other account containing the error.

Income tax and social security deductions are liabilities, payable to the tax authorities. If they have been recorded twice, the credit balance is too high, and the correction will need a debit entry in this account.

The contra entry has credited both the control accounts, and to correct this will require a debit entry in the account containing the error (the payables ledger control account).

Closing inventory should be a debit entry, and so a debit is needed to correct the error.

A balance for an accrual is a credit balance, but has been recorded incorrectly as a debit balance. To correct the error, the telephone expense account must be credited, and so the suspense account will be debited

263 A

To decide what entries are needed in the suspense account, you should think about the entry in the other account that is needed to correct the error. The entry in the suspense account is then the other side of the double entry. For example, inventory (an asset) should be a debit balance, so to correct the error we need to debit the inventory account and credit suspense account. Similarly, sales tax payable should be a credit balance, and to record the missing sales tax, we need to credit the sales tax account, debit suspense account.

Suspense account

	$		$
Balance (balancing figure)	2,050	Inventory (1,475 + 1,745)	3,220
Telephone expense (2 × $190)	380		
Sales tax ($5,390 – $4,600)	790		
	——		——
	3,220		3,220
	——		——

264 A

The sales tax balance for purchases should be a debit balance, because the money is recoverable from the tax authorities. The sale tax recoverable has been recorded as a credit entry (liability) instead of a debit entry, so to make the correction, we need to debit the sales tax account by 2 × $3,079 = $6,158. The correction is debit sales tax $6,158, credit suspense account $6,158.

265 B

If the suspense account shows a credit balance, the correcting entry to clear the account must be Debit Suspense account $130, credit the account with the error $130.

Purchases have been overstated by $130, and to correct this, we need to credit the Purchases account (and so debit Suspense account) with $130.

Omissions of transactions (item A and possibly item C) do not affect total debits and credits. If item C means that total accounts receivable have been reduced by the irrecoverable debt, but the irrecoverable debts account does not yet show the irrecoverable debt, the correcting entry would be to debit the Irrecoverable debts account and credit Suspense account. The error in item D leaves total debits and credits equal.

266 C

This is an error of principle because an expense item (motor repairs) has been charged to a non-current asset account.

267 A

The bookkeeper has omitted to record the income from the insurance claim. To record this, credit the insurance account (income = credit entry). The corresponding double entry is to the suspense account, because the other side of the double entry has already been correctly recorded in the cash account.

268 A

Income and liabilities are credit balances in the trial balance.

269 B

Assets, expenses and drawings are debit balances in the trial balance.

270 C

This question combines the fact that income and liabilities are credit balances in the trial balance and assets, expenses and drawings are debit balances.

271 B

Compensating errors can be difficult to find because similar numerical errors are made on both debits and credits.

272 B

The first mistake has no effect on the arithmetical aspect of the trial balance. A debit entry has been placed to another account with a debit balance. To correct the second error, the account payable must be credited with $200 to bring the balance to nil. Then the $200 must be credited to the account receivable, making a total adjustment of $400.

273 A

The invoice has been posted to the incorrect personal account.

274 D

The trial balance would indicate this situation where parts of double entry are omitted.

275 D

1st error. The transaction was not posted at all, therefore no debt and no credit entry. No imbalance in the trial balance.

2nd error. The discount received of $30 should be credited to the discounts received account, not debited. As a result, debit balances are $60 ($30 × 2) higher than credit balances.

3rd error. Cash drawings by the business owner should be recorded as debit Drawings, credit Cash/Bank. Here, the wrong account has been debited, but the debit entry amount is nevertheless the same as the credit entry amount, and the trial balance is unaffected.

Taking the three errors together, since total debits are higher than total credits by $60, the balance on the suspense account will be $60, to make total debits and total credits equal.

276 D

The trial balance is a list of balances and not part of the double entry system.

277 D

The purchase day book has been undercast by $500 (i.e. the total is $500 lower than it should be). As a result of this, the purchases account has been debited and the payables ledger control account credited with $500 too little.

The sales day book has been overcast by $700. As a result, the sales account has been credited and the receivable ledger control account has been debited with $700 too much.

As a result of these errors, the control account balances need to be adjusted, and profit reduced by ($500 + $700) $1,200, by reducing sales and increasing purchases.

Neither error affects the entries in the accounts of individual receivables and payables.

278 C

All non-routine asset purchases, such as those for non-current or long-term assets are first recorded in the journal.

279 A

The amount has been posted to the incorrect general ledger (nominal) account.

280 C

The trial balance is simply an indicator of arithmetical correctness.

Section 5

MOCK EXAM QUESTIONS AND ANSWERS

ANSWER ALL THE QUESTIONS

1   Kew has an overdraft of $4,400 at 1 June 20X5. The following four transactions occurred during June. Kew allows its customers up to 60 days to pay their invoices.

   3 June   Kew sold goods worth $10,000 on credit to a customer who always takes the full credit period.

   10 June   Kew paid a supplier $8,000.

   20 June   Kew made a cash sale of goods with a list price of $12,000 less 5% trade discount.

   23 June   Cash was received from a customer who has been in dispute with Kew. The original invoice was for $6,000, but Kew agreed to accept half the invoice value to settle the dispute.

   What was Kew's bank balance at 30 June 20X5?

   Ⓐ $2,000

   B $2,600

   C $10,800

   D $12,000

2   Victoria & Co wishes to buy goods from Paddington & Co.

   Which of the following is the most likely flow of documents to complete the purchase?

   A   Purchase order, delivery note, goods received note, cheque requisition, invoice

   Ⓑ   Purchase order, delivery note, goods received note, invoice, cheque requisition

   C   Goods received note, purchase order, delivery note, invoice, cheque requisition

   D   Purchase order, goods received note, delivery note, cheque requisition, invoice

3   Which of the following statements best explains the purpose of the journal?

Ⓐ   It is a record of all transactions included in the ledger accounts

B   It is a record of all cash transactions included in the ledger accounts   ✗

C   It is a record of all cash transactions included in the ledger accounts

Ⓓ   It is a record of all transactions included in the ledger accounts which have not been captured in other books of prime entry

4   Which of the following is NOT an effective security procedure?

A   A key must be inserted in to the cash register before it will operate. Keys are held by authorised personnel

Ⓑ   Cash is counted by a responsible person who works on the cash register

C   The cash reconciliation should be performed by a responsible person who neither operates the cash register nor counts the cash   ✓

D   Cash should be banked as promptly as possible

5   Which document lists the invoices, credit notes and amounts paid by a business and is issued by a supplier to customers, usually on a monthly basis?

A   Delivery note

B   Purchase order   ✓

C   Quotation

Ⓓ   Statement

6   Pimlico & Co owes Vauxhall for goods it recently purchased. Pimlico & Co are settling the invoice early and will pay the discounted amount.

What is the correct double entry for this in Pimlico & Co's books?

Ⓐ   Debit Vauxhall, Credit Bank, Credit Discount received

B   Debit Vauxhall, Debit Discount received, Credit Bank

C   Debit Bank, Credit Revenue, Credit Pimlico & Co

D   Debit Bank, Debit Revenue, Credit Pimlico & Co   ✓

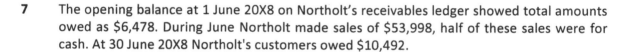

7   The opening balance at 1 June 20X8 on Northolt's receivables ledger showed total amounts owed as $6,478. During June Northolt made sales of $53,998, half of these sales were for cash. At 30 June 20X8 Northolt's customers owed $10,492.

How much cash did Northolt receive from its customers during June 20X8?

A $58,012

Ⓑ $49,984

C $31,013   ✗

Ⓓ $22,985

8 Sarah calculated that her cash book balance was a debit balance of $230 at 31 December 20X4, but her bank statement balance at that date was a different amount. Items that may affect the bank statement balance at that date were as follows:

(i) A cheque that Sarah paid into the bank for $250 was still outstanding

(ii) A cheque for $85 paid by Sarah to Molly had not yet been presented at the bank

(iii) Sarah had forgotten to record a cash withdrawal of $70

(iv) Sarah bank statement included bank charges of $25 which had been deducted from her account

What was the balance on Sarah's bank statement at 31 December 20X4?

Ⓐ $325

B $65

C $10 ✗

Ⓓ $30

9 **What legislation prevents the unnecessary retention of personal information?**

A Contract law

Ⓑ Data protection law ✓

C Document retention law

D Sale of goods legislation

10 **Which of the following is revenue expenditure in a business which has a large fleet of motor vehicles?**

(i) Purchase of a new delivery van

(ii) Redecorating the transport manager's office

(iii) Paying the road fund licenses for the fleet of vehicles

(iv) Purchase for a new exhaust for a van

A All four expenses

Ⓑ (ii), (iii) and (iv) ✓

C (i) and (ii)

D (iii) only

11 **What is the purpose of a remittance advice?**

A To pay a supplier

B To remind a customer to pay

Ⓒ To match a customer's payment with the invoices paid

D To send goods back to a supplier ✓

12 Which of the following will a bank refuse to accept?

A An unsigned cheque

B A crossed cheque made out to the person presenting it

C An account payee cheque paid in by the named person

D A large deposit of notes and coins

13 What are the accounting entries to record the transfer of surplus petty cash no longer required into the bank account of a business?

A Dr Bank, Cr Petty cash

B Dr Bank, Cr Sales

C Dr Sales, Cr Bank

D Dr Petty cash, Cr Bank

14 Which method of payment would be used to make an immediate internet purchase?

A Cash

B Cheque

C Credit card

D Credit transfer

15 Which of the following is capital expenditure?

A A debt owed to a supplier

B A bank loan

C The purchase cost of a new machine

D Employee salary costs

16 The following information has been extracted from a trader's wages records for April.

(i) Employees' pension contributions $783

(ii) Gross basic wages $10,163

(iii) Income tax $2,150

(iv) Employer's pension contributions $1,011

What will be the total charge for wages in the final accounts?

A $10,946

B $11,174

C $13,096

D $13,324

10,163 + 1,011

17   Which of the following categories of account would you expect to have a debit balance when you extract a trial balance from the nominal ledger?

(i)   Asset accounts

(ii)   Liability accounts

(iii)   Income accounts

(iv)   Expense accounts ✓

A   (i) and (iii)

Ⓑ   (i) and (iv)

C   (ii) and (iii)

D   (ii) and (iv)

18   The balance on an accounts payable control account at 1 April 20X5 was $18,420. During the month the business made purchases on credit of $27,400. Unpaid payables at 30 April 20X5 were $9,250. During April 20X5 credit notes amounting to $2,610 were received from suppliers.

What payments were made to accounts payables during April 20X5?

A $15,260

B $20,810

Ⓒ $33,960 ✓

D $39,180

19   The entries in an accounts receivable control account were as follows:

Balance brought forward	$3,500 –
Sales	$250,000 –
Bank	$225,000
Returns inwards	$2,500
Irrecoverable debts	$3,000

✓

What was the closing balance on the accounts receivable control account?

Ⓐ $23,000

B $25,500

C $26,000

D $28,000

[handwritten working:]
RCL
Balance b/d 3500   Bank 225,000
Sales 250,000   Returns 2,500
                 Debts 3,000
253,500   Balance c/d 23,000

20   Which of the following are used in determining irrecoverable debts?

A   An aged payables analysis

Ⓑ   An aged receivables analysis ✓

C   A bank statement

D   A supplier statement

21   **A business that is registered for sales tax purchases goods from a supplier. How would the purchase be recorded in the general ledger?**

Ⓐ   Debit Purchases, Credit Accounts payables, Credit sales tax

Ⓑ   Debit Purchases, Credit Accounts payables, Debit sales tax

C   Credit Purchases, Debit Accounts payables, Credit sales tax   ✗

D   Credit Purchases, Debit Accounts payables, Debit sales tax

22   **Which of the following is correct in relation to the trade receivables control account?**

(i)   The gross value of goods returned by credit customers is debited to the trade receivables control account.

(ii)   Trade discounts to credit customers are excluded from the trade receivables control account.

(iii)   Contras between the trade receivables' and trade payables' control accounts are debited to the trade receivables control account.

A   (i) and (ii) only

B   (i) only

Ⓒ   (ii) only   ✓

D   (ii) and (iii) only

23   A supplier of computer equipment allows its customers to deduct 3% from the invoice amount if they pay within 14 days of the invoice date.

What is this an example of?

A   An irrecoverable debt

B   A trade discount   ✓

C   A cash transaction

Ⓓ   An early settlement discount

24   Michael is a salesperson who is paid according to the number of sales he makes. His salary is a percentage of the gross sales.

By what method of remuneration is Michael paid?

A   Bonus

Ⓑ   Commission

C   Overtime   ✓

D   Salary

25 A summary of the transactions of Witney & Co, which is registered for sales tax at 17.5%, showed the following for the month of November 20X4:

Outputs of $122,610 (inclusive of sales tax) and Inputs of $78,857 (exclusive of sales tax)

At1 November 20X4, Witney owed sales tax of $7,200 and during November paid $6,800.

What is the balance of sales tax owing at 30 November 20X4?

- A $4,461
- B $4,861
- C $9,000
- D $9,400

26 Sally started in business as a sole trader, selling flowers. She introduced $2,200 of her savings into the business and her car, which is worth $750.

What journal entry is required to record this?

- A Debit Motor vehicles, Debit Bank, Credit Capital
- B Debit Motor vehicles, Credit Capital, Credit Bank
- C Debit Bank, Credit Motor Vehicles, Credit capital
- D Debit Capital, Credit Motor vehicles, Credit Bank

27 Which of the following documents would you NOT expect to come across in dealing with sales to customers?

- A Purchase order
- B Delivery note
- C Goods received note
- D Statement

28 Which of the following should be classified as assets in a business that sells scaffolding equipment?

- A Bank overdraft
- B Accounts receivable
- C Accounts payable
- D Bank loan –

29 Christina withdraws $300 from her business bank account for petty cash. How should this be recorded in the general ledger?

- A Debit Bank, Credit Petty cash
- B Debit Petty Cash, credit Bank
- C Debit Petty Cash, credit Capital
- D No record is necessary

30 Sock, a business registered for sales tax, purchased goods from a supplier for $6,000 plus sales tax of $1,050. Some of the goods were found to be faulty, and Sock returned one-third of the goods to the supplier. The supplier subsequently issued a credit note for the goods returned.

How should the credit note be recorded by Sock?

A   Debit Supplier account $2,000, Dr sales tax $350, Cr Purchases returns $2,350

B   Debit Supplier account $2,350, Cr Purchases returns $2,000, Cr Sales tax $350

C   Debit Purchases returns $2,000, Dr Sales tax $350, Credit Supplier account $2,350

D   Debit Purchases $2,350, Credit Supplier account $2,350   ✘

31 Which of the following errors would NOT be made using computerised accounts?

A   Error of commission

B   Error of principle

C   Omitting an entire transaction   ✔

D   Only completing one half of the double entry

32 What is an accounts receivable ledger?

A   An account for recording total sales

B   An account for recording the total of transactions with credit customers   ✔

C   A set of accounts for recording the transactions with individual credit customers

D   A set of accounts for recording the cash and credit transactions with individual customers

33 What is the double entry required to post the sales day book totals to the nominal ledger?

A   Debit Cash, Credit Sales

B   Debit Accounts receivable, Credit Sales   ✔

C   Debit Cash, Credit Sales

D   Debit Accounts receivable, Credit Cash

34 The following totals appear on a page of the purchases day book.

Total	Suppliers	Sales tax
$	$	$
5,657	4,865	792

What entry should be posted to the purchases account from the day book?

A   Debit Purchases $4,865

B   Debit Purchases $5,657

C   Credit Purchases $4,865   ✘

D   Credit Purchases $5,657

35 **For what reason does a business try to ensure a division of duties in the accounts department?**

A To reduce the risk of fraud

B To prevent individuals from being overworked

C To make supervision easier

D To improve the cover for absentees

36 Nigel has discovered a mistake in recording a sales return transaction from the sales returns day book to the nominal ledger. He had debited the accounts receivables account and credited the sales returns account.

Which book of prime entry should be used to record the correction of the error?

A Sales returns day book

B Journal

C Cash book

D Sales day book

37 **Which of the following is a secure form of paying salaries in a large organisation?**

A BACS

B Cash

C Standing order

D Direct debit

38 **Terry has bought a car on credit for his business. Which components of the accounting equation will change as a result of this transaction?**

A Assets and capital

B Capital and liabilities

C Assets and liabilities

D Assets, capital and liabilities

39 **What is the impact upon the net assets of a business when an expense is incurred but not yet paid?**

A The net assets of the business remain unchanged

B The net assets of the business will be reduced

C The net assets of the business will be increased

D It is not possible to determine the impact upon net assets without further information

40   Fork Co offers its credit customers a settlement discount of 5% for payment within 10 days of the invoice date. Fork Co is preparing an invoice for a credit customer who purchased goods with a list price of $1,000. This customer is also eligible for 10% trade discount. It is highly probable that the customer will take advantage of the early settlement terms and pay within 10 days.

What will be the total due on the invoice sent to the customer?

A $1,000 $1000 × 0.95 = 950

B $900

C $855   950 × 0.90 = 855   ✓

D $950

41   **After carrying out a bank reconciliation, which of the following items could require an entry in the cash book?**

(i)   Credit transfers shown in the bank statement

(ii)   Dishonoured cheque

A   Item (i) only

B   Item (ii) only -

C   Items (i) and (ii)   ✗

D   Neither (i) nor (ii)

42   **Which of the following statements is true?**

A   Cash purchases are credited to the purchases account.

B   Cash sales are debited to the sales revenue account.   ✓

C   Settlement discounts received are debited to the trade payables control account.

D   Settlement discounts received re credited to the trade payables control account.

43   **In reconciling a business cash book with the bank statement, which of the following items could require a subsequent entry in the cash book?**

Errors:

1   Cheques presented after the date of the bank statement
2   A cheque from a customer that has been dishonoured
3   An error by the bank
4   Bank charges
5   Deposits credited after the date of the bank statement
6   Standing order payment entered in the bank statement

A   Items 2, 3, 4 and 6 only

B   Items 1, 2, 5 and 6 only

C   Items 2, 4 and 6 only   ✓

D   Items 1, 3 and 5 only

44 Knife Co offers its credit customers a settlement discount of 10% for payment within 10 days of the invoice date. Knife Co is preparing an invoice for a credit customer who has purchased goods for $2,000. This customer is also eligible for 5% trade discount. It is highly probable that the customer will not take advantage of the early settlement terms and pay after 30 days in accordance with normal credit terms.

What will be the total due on the invoice sent to the customer?

A $2,000

B $1,800

C $1,900

D $1,710

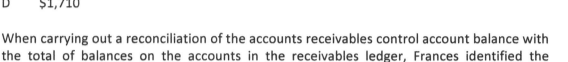

2000 × 0.95 = 1900   ✓

45 When carrying out a reconciliation of the accounts receivables control account balance with the total of balances on the accounts in the receivables ledger, Frances identified the following two errors.

(i)   In the sales day book for one day, the total was overcast by $560. (The total was added up incorrectly, and was too high by $560.)

(ii)   A total of $830 of receipts in the cash book had been entered in the receivables' ledger control account as $380.

By how much did the balance on the accounts receivable control account differ from the total of the individual receivables ledger account balances?

A   The accounts receivable control account balance was higher than the total of the ledger account balances by $110.

B   The accounts receivable control account balance was higher than the total of the ledger account balances by $1,010.

C   The accounts receivable control account balance was lower than the total of the ledger account balances by $110.

D   The accounts receivable control account balance was lower than the total of the ledger account balances by $1,010.

✗

Error (i) RCA was too high by 560

Error (ii) Payments from AR understated by (830-380)   450

Balance on receivables control a/c too high by: 1,010

46 Dan is a trainee accountant. He has made the following attempt at a bank reconciliation statement.

	$
Overdraft in the bank statement	43,700
Add: deposits not credited by the bank	52,900
	96,600
Less: outstanding cheques to suppliers	7,800
Overdraft in the cash book	88,800

What is the correct balance on the cash book?

A $88,800 overdraft, as stated

B $17,000 overdraft

C $1,400 overdraft

D $1,400 cash in bank

47 Which pair of the following account balances would you expect to appear on the same side of a trial balance?

A   Purchases and petty cash

B   Office equipment and accounts payable

C   Accounts receivables and sales

D   Telephone expenses and accounts payable

48 William operates an imprest system for petty cash, and the float in petty cash is topped up to $250 at the end of each month.

During April, $25 was paid into petty cash by employees paying for private use of the office photocopier and a cheque for $20 was cashed for an employee out of petty cash. During April, cheques for $340 were drawn by William for petty cash.

How much cash was paid out for petty cash expenses during April?

A $295

B $345

C $355

D $385

(25-20) + 340

49 A business has an accounts receivable control account and an accounts payable control account in its general ledger. A trial balance has been extracted, but the debit and credit totals are not equal.

Which of the following errors might be the cause of this failure to balance?

A   The purchase of a new computer has been debited to the computer repairs and maintenance account.

B   A cheque from Crow, who is also a supplier to the business, has been credited to the accounts payable ledger account of Crow.

C   Sales returned by Jackdaw have been debited to the accounts receivable ledger account of Jackdaw.

(D)   The cost of purchasing new telephone equipment has been credited to the telephone expenses account.   ✓

50 A business has an opening balance on the sales tax account showing a receivable of $590 and a closing balance also showing a receivable of $460. During the period there were standard rated outputs of $4,200 and standard rated inputs of $6,000 both exclusive of sales tax. The standard rate of sales tax is 17.5%.

How much was the sales tax repayment received during the period?

A $185

(B) $445

(C) $1,365   ✗

D $1,930

Sales Tax Account

Balance	590	Output tax	735
Input tax	1050	Sales tax repayment	445
		Closing bal	460
	1640		1640

33/50
= 66%

MOCK EXAM ANSWERS

1   A

		$
1 June	Opening overdraft	(4,400)
10 June	Pay supplier	(8,000)
20 June	Cash sale ($12,000 less 5%)	11,400
23 June	Cash from customer	3,000
		_____
30 June	Closing balance	2,000
		_____

2   B

Document	Produced by:
Purchase order	Victoria & Co
Delivery note	Supplier
Goods received note	Victoria & Co
Invoice	Supplier
Cheque requisition	Victoria & Co

3   D

A journal is used to record or capture transactions not included in other books of prime entry.

4   B

It is not an effective security procedure for the person who takes the cash from customers to count it at the end of the day. It opens up a possibility of theft/fraud.

5   D

The other documents are used in purchases and sales. The statement contains financial transactions.

6   A

For example, if a business pays a supplier's invoice of $1,000 by sending a cheque for $950 and taking a $50 settlement discount, the payment transaction would be recorded as:

Debit: Accounts payable $1,000

Credit: Bank $950

Credit: Discounts received $50

7   B

	$
Opening accounts receivable	6,478
Credit sales in June (50% of $53,998)	26,999
	33,477
Closing accounts receivable	(10,492)
Therefore cash from accounts receivable in June	22,985
Cash from cash sales (50% of $53,998)	26,999
Total cash received from customers	49,984

8   D

The $30 balance is an overdraft balance.

	$		$
Sally's recorded bank balance	230	Updated cash book balance	135
Cash withdrawal omitted	(70)	Cheque paid in, not yet cleared	(250)
Bank charges	(25)	Cheque payment to Molly, not yet presented	85
Updated cash book balance	135	Bank statement balance	(30)

9   B

This prevents businesses holding personal information without legitimate reason.

10   B

Revenue expenditure includes redecorating work in buildings, vehicle running costs and repairs and maintenance. Only the purchase of a van is capital expenditure.

11   C

A customer issues a remittance advice with the payment of an invoice. This allows the person receiving the payment to match the payment with the invoice.

12   A

A cheque must be signed by an authorised signatory. Without a signature the cheque is not an authority to pay. The bank might query a large amount of notes if tendered by someone unknown, in case the money had the potential of coming from criminal activity.

13 A

The bank account will increase (debit entry) and petty cash will be reduced (credit entry).

14 C

A credit card enables a purchaser to make an immediate payment on a secure server.

15 C

The debt to the supplier and the bank loan are both liabilities and labour costs are revenue expenditure.

16 B

The amount charged to the accounts comprises the gross wages and the employer's pension contributions. Employees' pension contributions and income tax are deducted from the gross basic wages.

17 B

We should expect debit balances on asset and expense accounts, and credit balances on liability, capital and income accounts.

18 C

	$
Opening payables balance	18,420
Credit purchases	27,400
	45,820
Credit notes received	(2,610)
	43,210
Closing payables balance	(9,250)
Payments to accounts payable	33,960

19 A

Accounts receivable control account

	$		$
Balance b/d	3,500	Bank	225,000
Sales	250,000	Sales returns	2,500
		Irrecoverable debts	3,000
		Balance c/d	23,000
	253,500		253,500

20   B

The aged accounts receivable analysis lists outstanding accounts receivable in terms of amount and length of time outstanding which are useful guides in determining when an outstanding debt becomes an irrecoverable debt.

21   B

For example, if a business purchases an item for $1,000 plus sales tax at $175, the ledger entries should be:

Debit Purchases	$1,000
Debit Sales tax	$175
Credit Accounts payable	$1,175

22   C

Trade discounts should be deducted before the invoice is prepared; therefore, they are excluded from the trade receivables control account. The remaining two statements (i) and (iii) are false. The gross value of goods returned inwards by credit customers will be credited (not debited) to the trade receivables control account to reduce the balance outstanding. Contras between the trade receivables' and trade payables' control accounts are accounted for as follows: Debit Trade payables' control account, Credit Trade receivables' control account.

23   D

A trade discount is a discount agreed at the time the sale is made. Examples are bulk purchase discounts for sales orders above a certain size, and discounts to regular customers. A discount offered for early payment is referred to as a settlement discount or a cash discount.

24   B

Commission is percentage-based remuneration which is designed to motivate success.

25   B

Sales tax account

	$		$
Bank	6,800	Opening balance b/f	7,200
Payables/bank (input tax)	13,800	Receivables/cash (output tax)	18,261
Closing balance c/f	4,861		
	———		———
	25,461		25,461
	———		———
		Balance b/f	4,861

Tax on sales (outputs) = (17.5/117.5) × $122,610 = $18,261.

Tax on purchases = 17.5% × $78,857 = $13,800.

26   A

Debit Motor vehicles	$750
Debit Bank	$2,200
Credit Capital	$2,950

27   C

A goods received note is prepared by the purchaser after the goods have been delivered, for internal use only. The supplier receives a purchase order from the customer, provides a delivery note on delivery of the goods, and might issue periodic statements to customers.

28   B

Accounts receivable are a business asset. Accounts payable, bank overdrafts and bank loans are all liabilities.

29   B

The money is being added to petty cash, therefore debit the petty cash account (asset account). The money is being taken from the bank; therefore reduce the bank balance by crediting the bank account.

30   B

The credit note will include sales tax on the returns – this should be accounted for.

31   D

An error of commission is quite easy to make using a computerised system because it is quite easy to select an incorrect code. The same can be said of an error of principle. It is equally possible to omit items in both manual and computerised systems.

32   C

The accounts receivable ledger is a set of accounts for 'account customers'. These are credit customers, and each customer has an individual account in the ledger.

33   B

The sales day book records credit sales to customers. The total in the day book is transferred to the general ledger as a debit to total accounts receivable and a credit to the sales account. The invoices sent to each individual credit customer are also transferred, as debit entries in the individual accounts of the customers in the receivables ledger.

34   A

The transfer to the purchases account (debit entry for an expense) should exclude sales tax.

35   A

Division of duties means that one person is able to check the work done by someone else. This builds in a check, so that errors and fraud are more easily detected.

36   B

The journal is the book of prime entry that is used to record the correction of errors in the accounts.

37   A

BACS is an electronic system of payment and is far more secure than holding cash on the premises for wages. Standing orders and direct debits are used by customers to pay amounts to suppliers of goods and, more frequently, services.

38   C

The car is an asset and accounts payable are liabilities. There is no impact on profit.

39   B

When an expense is incurred, profit will be reduced, which will result in a reduction in the net assets of the business. This will be reflected in the statement of financial position by inclusion of a liability to reflect the amount still to be paid.

40   C

Trade discount is always deducted prior to the invoice being prepared. Settlement discount is also deducted when it is highly probable that the customer will take advantage of the early settlement discount terms.

	$
Sale price	1,000.00
Less: trade discount (10%)	(100.00)
	900.00
Less: settlement discount (5%)	(45.00)
Invoice amount	855.00

41   C

Credit transfers might not be entered in the cash book until they are notified to the business by a bank statement. Similarly, dishonoured cheques might not be recorded in the cash book until they are reported in a bank statement.

42   C

Settlement discount received from suppliers are debited to the trade payables control account to reduce the remaining balance outstanding to credit suppliers.

43 C

Items shown in the bank statement that should subsequently be recorded in the cash book are items that the business does not learn about until it receives the bank statement. These include bank charges, dishonoured cheques and standing orders and direct debit payments.

44 C

Trade discount is always deducted prior to the invoice being prepared. Settlement discount is only deducted when it is highly probable that the customer will take advantage of the early settlement discount terms. As this customer is not expected to take advantage of the settlement discount terms, settlement discount is not deducted.

	$
Sale price	2,000.00
Less: trade discount (5%)	(100.00)
Invoice amount	1,900.00

45 B

	$
Error (i): Balance on receivables control account too high by:	560
Error (ii): Payments from accounts receivable under-stated by (830 – 380)	450
Balance on receivables control account too high by:	1,010

46 D

	$
Bank statement balance	(43,700)
Not yet processed by the bank:	
Cheques from customers	52,900
Cheques to suppliers	(7,800)
Cash book balance	1,400

47 A

Purchases are an expense item and therefore a debit balance. Petty cash is an asset and therefore a debit balance.

48   B

	$
Balance at start of month	250
Payments into petty cash for photocopying	25
Cash to employee	(20)
	255
Cheques drawn for petty cash	340
	595
Balance at end of month	(250)
Therefore petty cash expenditure	345

49   D

When a trial balance fails to balance, with total debit balances and total credit balances being unequal, one or more errors must have occurred in which there has not been a matching debit and credit entry in two nominal ledger accounts. Item A is an error, but the cost of the new computer has been debited to the wrong account, and there is no difference between total debits and total credits as a result. Items B and C are both errors, but these affect individual customer and supplier accounts in the receivables ledger and the payables ledger: they do not affect nominal ledger account balances. Item D is an item that should be debited to an equipment (long term asset) account, but has been credited to an account in error. This causes total debits and total credits to be unequal.

50   B

Sales tax account

	$		$
Opening balance	590	Output tax ($4,200 × 0.175)	735
Input tax ($6,000 × 0.175)	1,050	Sales tax repayment (β)	445
		Closing balance	460
	1,640		1,640

Section 6

SPECIMEN EXAM QUESTIONS

Section A – ALL 50 questions are compulsory and MUST be attempted

Each question is worth 2 marks.

1   Which of the following is an example of capital expenditure?

    A   Paying for refurbishment as part of upgrading a building

    B   Paying carriage outwards in respect of selling goods

    C   Paying legal fees in order to recover customer debts

    D   Paying bonuses to production operatives

2   Vic's receivables ledger balances total $50,000, which does not agree with his trade receivables control account. The following errors were found:

    (a)   A credit note for $750 was not recorded in the receivables ledger

    (2)   A contra entry of $2,000 was entered in the control account but not in the receivables and payables ledgers.

    What should be the total of the balances on his receivables ledger after correcting the following errors?

    A $52,750

    B $50,000

    C $49,250

    D $47,250

3   Christa pays her mortgage by instructing her bank to make monthly payments of a fixed amount from her current account. When the mortgage rate changes Christa issues a revised instruction to the bank.

    Which method of payment is Christa using?

    A   Standing Order

    B   Payable Order

    C   Direct Debit

    D   Crossed cheque

4 A firm has a credit facility with a local trade supplier. An invoice for purchases has been credited to the supplier's account and debited to the sales account.

Which of the following journal entries will correct the error?

A   Dr Sales account   Cr Supplier account

B   Dr Supplier account   Cr Sales account

Ⓒ   Dr Purchases account   Cr Sales account   ✓

D   Dr Sales account   Cr Bank account

5 **Which of the following would be on the debit side of the payables ledger control account?**

1   Cash paid

2   Irrecoverable debts

3   Discounts received

4   Purchases

A   1, 2 and 3 only

B   2 and 4 only   ✓

Ⓒ   1 and 3 only

D   1, 2, 3 and 4

6 The following is a summary of the petty cash transactions for a week:

Income	$	Expenditure	$
Opening balance	500	Travelling expenses	150
Sale of stamps	10	Subsistence expenses	250
Sale of paper	50		

Petty cash is maintained using the imprest system.

What sum should be reclaimed by the cashier at the end of the week?

Ⓐ $160

Ⓑ $340

C $400   ✗

D $500

7 **The balance on the payables ledger control account should be equal to which other figure in the accounting system?**

A   The total of the balances on the individual customers' accounts

Ⓑ   The total of the balances on the individual suppliers' accounts   ✓

C   The unreconciled balance on the receivables ledger control account

D   The balance on the receivables ledger control account reconciled for items in transit

8   Louise introduces her car into her business.

Which parts of the business' accounting equation will change?

A   Assets and capital

B   Capital and profit

C   Liabilities and assets

D   Capital and liabilities

9   Freya started in business on 1 September. During September she made cash sales of $6,400 and issued credit sales invoices for $10,200 of which $8,600 had been paid.

What would be the balance of the sales account in the general ledger at the end of September?

A $6,400

B $10,200

C $8,000

D $16,600

10   **Which of the following journal entries correctly records the credit purchase of plant and equipment?**

A   Dr Payables ledger control account   Cr Plant and Equipment

B   Dr Cash   Cr Plant and Equipment

C   Dr Plant and Equipment   Cr Payables ledger control account

D   Dr Plant and Equipment   Cr Cash

11   Marvin has a balance of $3,350 on his receivables ledger control account but his list of customer balances totals $3,500.

Which of the following balances would explain the difference?

A   The total of sales day book was overstated by $150

B   A contra of $150 has been posted in the customer's individual account but not the control account

C   A credit note of $150 has not been recorded in the sales day book

D   An irrecoverable debt has been accounted for in the control account but not the individual customer account

12 Albert sold 15 units of inventory with a list price of $40 per unit to Michael. He gives Michael a 10% trade discount and also a 5% settlement discount if Michael pays within 30 days. Based upon previous experience, Michael never pays early to take advantage of settlement discount offered.

What will be the total of the invoice that Albert issues to Michael for this transaction?

A $540

B $600

C $510 ✓

D $513

13 **Which of the following errors would be found by extracting a trial balance?**

A A transaction has been completely missed in the accounts

B The double entries have been made the wrong way round ✓

C Different figures have been entered for the debit and credit entries

D An expense item has been posted to a non-current asset account.

14 Dion performed a payables' ledger control account reconciliation and found the following errors:

(1) The purchase day book was overstated by $720

(2) A credit note for $380 was omitted from the day books altogether

Which of the following shows the necessary adjustments to ensure that the balances reconcile at the correct amount?

A Dr Payables ledger control account $1,100, Subtract $380 from the list of supplier balances ✗

B Dr Payables ledger control account $1,100, Add $380 to the list of supplier balances

C Cr Payables ledger control account $1,100, Subtract $380 from the list of supplier balances

D Cr Payables ledger control account $1,100, Add $380 to the list of supplier balances

15 **Which of the following are benefits of an effective document retention policy to a small business?**

1 To ensure all documents are stored forever

2 To meet legal and tax requirements of the business

3 To mitigate risks arising from internal and external disputes of the business

4 To increase operational efficiency and maintain control over costs

A 1 and 3 only

B 2, 3 and 4 only ✓

C 1, 2 and 4 only

D 1, 2, 3 and 4

16 Hywel purchased goods on credit with a list price of $100. The supplier gave Hywel a trade discount of 10%. Sales tax is charged at 20% and both Hywel and the supplier are registered for sales tax.

What is the amount that Hywel will debit to his purchases account?

A $88.00

Ⓑ $90.00

Ⓒ $108.00

D $110.00

 ✗ (100 − 10% of 100)

17 **Which of the following are valid reasons for keeping a payables ledger control account?**

(1)   To obtain a figure for payables to be included in the statement of financial position

(2)   To assist in the location of errors

(3)   To check the accuracy of entries made in personal accounts

A   1 and 2 only

B   2 and 3 only

Ⓒ   1, 2 and 3    ✓

D   1 and 3 only

18 A credit sale of goods for $51 to J Davis was entered in the accounts as $15.

What type of error has occurred?

A   Compensating error

B   Error of omission   ✓

C   Error of principle

Ⓓ   Error of transposition

19 **Which of the following represents the correct imprest amount in an imprest petty cash system?**

A   Notes and coins in the cash box – vouchers for payments – IOUs

B   Notes and coins in the cash box + vouchers for payments – IOUs

C   Notes and coins in the cash box – vouchers for payments + IOUs   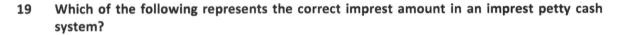 ✓

Ⓓ   Notes and coins in the cash box + vouchers for payments + IOUs

20 Which of the following statements are true about a good coding system for financial transactions?

1   It enables a company to easily extract data for management analysis

2   It provides a unique code for each item within the system

3   It provides codes that are uniform in format

4   It requires management authorisation before creation of new codes

A   1 and 2 only

B   3 and 4 only

C   2, 3 and 4 only

(D)   1, 2, 3 and 4

21 Which of the following is the correct posting from the purchase day book?

(A)   Dr Purchases account   Cr Payables ledger control account

B   Dr Purchases account   Cr Cash book

C   Dr Payables ledger control account   Cr Purchases account

D   Dr Cash book   Cr Purchases account

22 Annabel's cash book shows her to be $2,030 overdrawn. A bank reconciliation, however, shows that a standing order payment for $365 had been entered in the cash book twice, and that a dishonoured customer's cheque for $275 had been debited in the cash book rather than credited.

What is Annabel's true overdraft position?

A $1,845

(B) $1,940

C $2,120

(D) $2,215

-2030 - 550 + 365

23 Narvinda buys goods from Jamal for $2,500. He returns half of the goods on 15 May.

Which of the following documents would be issued by Jamal for the return of the goods?

A   Invoice

(B)   Credit note

C   Debit note

D   Remittance advice

24 If a cheque is marked 'Account Payee Only, Not Negotiable' what does this mean?

A   The cheque should be paid only into the account of the named drawer

(B)   The cheque should be paid only into the account of the named payee

C   The paying bank can deposit the cheque in an account other than the payee

D   The receiving bank can deposit the cheque in an account other than the payee

25   The following statements relate to the aged receivables analysis:

1   It provides information about debt collection efficiency to the management

2   It identifies when payments are due to be made to suppliers

Which of the above statements are correct?

A   1 only

B   2 only

C   Both the statements

D   Neither of the statements

26   **A credit entry into a ledger account represents which of the following?**

A   Increase in an expense

B   Increase in income

C   Increase in an asset

D   Increase in drawings

27   Iwan's payables ledger showed that $2,300 was owed to suppliers at the start of the week. During the week Iwan made purchases of $3,900 although he paid $900 of this in cash. He also paid suppliers $1,000 by cheque.

What is the closing balance on his payables ledger?

A $4,000

B $4,300

C $5,200

D $6,100

$(2300 + 3000) - 1000$

28   **Which of the following errors will require an entry to a suspense account to correct it?**

A   A credit purchase was completely omitted from the accounting records

B   A credit sale was recorded as a cash sale

C   The payment of wages was debited to the rent account instead of the wages account

D   The cash sale was recorded correctly in the sales account and credited in the bank account

29   **What document is usually sent every month from the supplier to the customer, listing all the transactions between them during that month?**

A   Invoice

B   Receipt

C   Statement

D   Credit note

30 A company has the following year end payroll information

Gross salaries and wages	$285,350
Income tax deducted	$61,063
Employers' pension contributions	$26,786
Employees' pension contributions	$23,034

What is the company's total payroll cost for the year?

(A) $312,136

B $274,107

C $396,233

D $308,384

31 Walter sells goods to Ninevah with a list price (exclusive of sales tax) of $4,300, offering a 4% trade discount. Walter is registered to account for sales tax and the rate of sales tax is 17.5%

What amount should be recorded for this transaction in Walter's sales account (to the nearest $1)?

(A) $4,850

(B) $4,128

C $5,053

D $3,513

4300 - 4% of 4300

32 **Which of the following statements regarding sales tax in the trial balance is true?**

A Output tax and input tax are debit balances

B Output tax and input tax are credit balances

(C) Output tax is a credit balance and input tax is a debit balance

D Output tax is a debit balance and input tax is a credit balance

33 **Which of the following should be classified as current liabilities?**

1 Trade receivables

2 Sales tax payable

3 Trade payables

4 Drawings

A 1 and 2

(B) 2 and 3

C 3 and 4

(D) 2 and 4

34 Sally's balance in her cash book is $160 debit. However her bank statement shows a different amount. On investigation, Sally discovered the following:

1 A cheque that Sally paid into the bank for $40 is still outstanding

2 A cheque for $60 paid by Sally to Molly has not yet been presented

3 Sally has forgotten to record a cash withdrawal of $30

4 When Sally inspects her bank statement she sees that the bank has deducted charges of $15 from her account

What is the balance on Sally's bank statement?

(A) $95

(B) $135

C $185

D $225

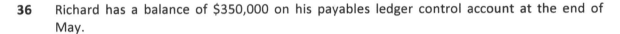

35 Avalon gives his customers individual trade discounts from the list price and also offers a 5% early settlement discount for all invoices settled within seven days of issue. A new customer, Novala, negotiated a 25% trade discount. Novala is not expected to take advantage of the settlement discount terms offered. Novala's transactions during June were:

12 June   Bought goods with a $5,000 list price

15 June   Returned goods with a $1,000 list price as faulty

16 June   Paid half of the net balance on its account

How much does Nolava owe Avalon at 30 June?

A $1,425

(B) $1,500

C $2,000

D $2,850

36 Richard has a balance of $350,000 on his payables ledger control account at the end of May.

What does this mean?

A He has bought $350,000 of goods in May

B He is owed $350,000 by his customers

(C) He owes $350,000 to his suppliers

D He has paid $350,000 to his suppliers in May

37   Melanie is a sales tax registered trader. Her purchases day book shows purchases of $2,000, net of sales tax at 17.5%.

What double entry will Melanie post at the end of her day's trading?

A   Dr Purchases $2,000   Cr Payables $2,000

B   Dr Purchases $2,350   Cr Payables $2,350   ✓

C   Dr Payables $2,350   Cr Purchases $2,000   Cr Sales tax $350

D   Dr Purchases $2,000   Dr Sales tax $350   Cr Payables $2,350

38   Seb packs goods on an assembly line. He is paid a different amount each week, depending on his output of assembled goods.

By what method of remuneration is Seb paid?

A   Piecework

B   Commission   ✓

C   Hourly rate

D   Salaried

39   The following ledger balances make up a company's trial balance:

	$
Sales	76,700
Purchases	26,800
Non-current assets	31,400
Payables	18,200
Receivables	32,300
Cash at bank	14,200
Capital	9,800

What is the total of the debit column of the trial balance?

A $94,900

B $104,700   ✓

C $105,900

D $209,400

40 Susan is a computer equipment dealer. She uses the following coding system for her financial transactions:

1st number	2nd number
100 Purchases	300 Cash
200 Sales	400 Payables
	500 Receivables

Danielle buys computer equipment worth $2,000 on credit from Susan.

Which of the following would be the code recorded on the invoice issued by Susan?

A   100300

B   100400

C   200300

D   200500

41 In Dalveer's cash receipts book for the month of June the trade receivables column totalled $6,570.

What does this amount represent?

A   The amount invoiced to Dalveer's customers during June

B   The amount owed by Dalveer's customers at the end of June

C   The amount received from Dalveer's customers during June

D   The value of cash sales during June

42 Jenny has a bank balance of $550 at the start of the week. During the week the following transactions occurred:

Day 1   She sold goods on credit for $876

Day 2   She received a cheque for $400 from a credit customer

Day 3   She purchased office equipment with a list price of $1,000 but received a 10% discount for paying immediately by cheque

How much does Jenny have in the bank at the end of the week?

A $2,826

B $400

C $50

D $126

43   Which of the following are books of prime entry?

    1   Sales day book

    2   Payables ledger

    3   Journal

    4   Cash book

    A   1, 3 and 4

    B   1, 2 and 4

    C   2, 3 and 4

    D   1, 2 and 3

44   Vauxhall recently sold goods on credit to Pimlico. Vauxhall does not expect Pimlico to take advantage of settlement discount offered for early payment of the invoice. However, Pimlico subsequently does pay early and is entitled to pay the reduced amount.

What is the correct double entry for settlement of the amount due in Vauxhall's books?

A	Dr Vauxhall	Cr Bank	Cr Discount received
B	Dr Vauxhall	Dr Discount received	Cr Bank
C	Dr Bank	Cr Revenue	Cr Pimlico
D	Dr Bank	Dr Revenue	Cr Pimlico

45   Fred works on a car factory assembly line and is paid a rate of $4.50/hour for a 35 hour week. All overtime is paid at time and a half. In addition a piecework rate of $25 for every car assembled each week is paid.

Last week Fred worked 46 hours and completed the assembly of three cars.

How much is Fred's gross pay for the week?

    A $282.00

    B $256.75

    C $306.75

    D $385.50

46   Which of the following will help to reduce overdue balances in receivables ledger accounts?

    A   Improved debt collection methods

    B   An increase in the bank overdraft facility

    C   Credit customers paying invoices more slowly

    D   An increase in credit facilities to customers

47 Carion sells the following goods for cash during January:

		Net Price $	Sales Tax $
5 Jan	To Maurice	386	68
19 Jan	To Harris	715	125
28 Jan	To Merton	430	75

What are the correct entries in Carion's general ledger?

A   Dr Sales $1,799   Dr Sales tax $268   Cr Cash $2,067

B   Dr Cash $2,067   Cr Sales $1,799   Cr Sales tax $268   ✓

C   Dr Sales $1,531   Dr Sales tax $268   Cr Cash $1,799 –

D   Dr Cash $1,799   Cr Sales $1,531   Cr Sales tax $268

48 **What journal entry would be posted if a sole trader starts a business by introducing his cash savings and a car into the business?**

A   Dr Motor vehicles   Dr Bank   Cr Capital -

B   Dr Bank   Cr Motor vehicles   Cr Bank   ✓

C   Dr Capital   Cr Motor vehicles   Cr Bank

D   Dr Motor vehicles   Cr Capital   Cr Bank -

49 Malindra sent a payment to Nicholas along with a document detailing the items and invoices the payment related to.

What is this document known as?

A   Debit note

B   Credit note   ✓

C   Remittance advice

D   Delivery note

50 The following statements relate to the receivables ledger control account:

1   Settlement discounts received will not be recorded in the trade receivables ledger control account

2   The allowance for the irrecoverable debts is recorded in the trade receivables ledger control account

Which of the above statements are true?

A   1 only

B   2 only   ✗

C   Both 1 and 2

D   Neither 1 nor 2

76%

(Total: 100 marks)

Section 7

ANSWERS TO SPECIMEN EXAM QUESTIONS

1   **A**

2   **D**

      ($50,000 − 750 − 2,000)

3   **A**

4   **C**

5   **C**

6   **B**

      ($250 + 150 − (50 + 10))

7   **B**

8   **A**

9   **D**

      ($10,200 + 6,400)

10   **C**

11   **D**

12   **A**

      ($15 × 40) − (10% of 600)

      As settlement discount is unlikely to be taken by Michael, this is ignored when the sales invoice is prepared.

13   C

14   A

15   B

16   B

($100 – 10% of 100)

Only the net purchase cost is debited to the purchases account. The sales tax charged on the purchase invoice will be debited to the sales tax account. The gross amount is credited to the payables ledger control account.

17   C

18   D

19   D

20   D

21   A

22   D

(– $2,030 – $550 + $365)

23   B

24   B

25   A

26   B

27   B

($2,300 + $3,000 – $1,000)

28   D

29   C

30 **A**

($285,350 + $26,786)

31 **B**

($4,300 – 4% of 4,300)

32 **C**

33 **B**

34 **B**

($160 – $40 + $60 – $30 – $15)

35 **B**

½ of ($4,000 – 25% of $4,000)

36 **C**

37 **D**

38 **A**

39 **B**

($26,800 + $31,400 + $32,300 + $14,200)

40 **D**

41 **C**

42 **C**

($950 – $(1,000 – 10% of 1,000)

43 **A**

44 **D**

As Pimlico was not expected to take advantage of the settlement discount offered, initial recording of the sale and receivable is not adjusted for settlement discount. When early settlement is subsequently made by Pimlico, the receivable in Vauxhall's nominal ledger is cleared by the receipt of cash and a reduction in revenue.

45 **C**

($4.50 × 35) + ($6.75 × 11) + (3 × $25)

46 **A**

47 **D**

48 **A**

49 **C**

50 **D**

Settlement discount received is recorded in the trade payables ledger control account. The allowance for receivables is maintained in a separate general ledger account. It is not part of the trade receivables ledger control account.